At the End of
the Final Line

To Raymond.
hope you enjoy
the story

Patrick Campbell

23 Jan 07

At the End of the Final Line

A Brief History of Aircraft Manufacturing at Canadian Vickers and Canadair from 1923 to 1984

Patrick J. Campbell

Shoreline

The original text by Patrick Campbell was used in *Canadair: the First 50 Years*, by Ron Pickler and Larry Milberry, Toronto: CANAV Books, 1995.

Photographs in *At the End of the Final Line* provided by the author.
Cover design and graphics, Sarah Robinson
Map lettering, Peter Smeets

Printed in Canada by Marquis Imprimeur
Published by Shoreline, 23 Ste-Anne
Ste-Anne-de-Bellevue, QC, Canada H9X 1L1
Phone/fax: 514-457-5733
shoreline@sympatico.ca www.shorelinepress.ca

Dépôt legal: Library and Archives Canada
et la Bibliothèque et Archives nationales du Québec

A first edition of this work was published in a 1994 limited printing.

Library and Archives Canada Cataloguing in Publication

Campbell, P. J. (Patrick J.), 1923-
At the end of the final line:
a brief history of aircraft manufacturing
at Canadian Vickers and Canadair
from 1923 to 1984 / Patrick J. Campbell.

ISBN 1-896754-49-X
1. Canadian Vickers Limited--History.
2. Canadair Limited--History.
3. Aircraft industry--Canada--History--
20th century. I. Title.

HD9711.C34C35 2005
338.7'62913334'09710904
C2005-904264-8

DEDICATION

This book is dedicated, most respectfully,
to the thousands of hourly-rated men and
women who worked long shifts in the
Maisonneuve and St. Laurent factories of
Canadian Vickers and Canadair.

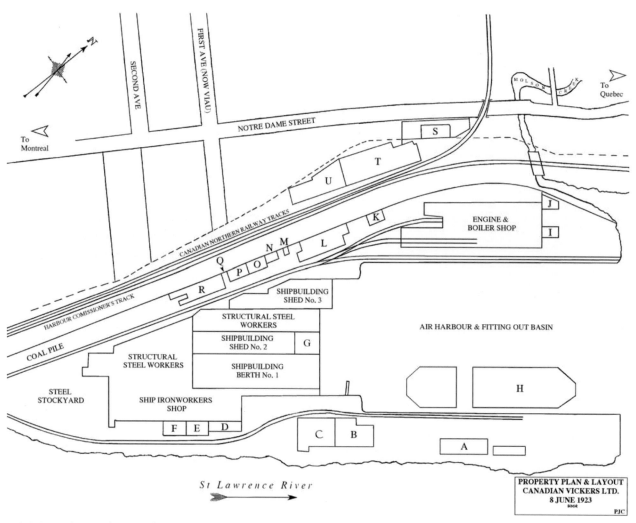

1. Map of Canadian Vickers, 8 June 1923

Map of Canadian Vickers, 1923

A. Machine shop
B. Sawmill
C. Joiners' shop, aeroplanes and Sea-Sleds*
D. Foreman's offices
E. Rivet store
F. Air compressor
G. Aircraft assembling
H. 'Duke of Connaught' floating drydock
I. Engineers' stores
J. Coppersmiths
K. Plumbers
L. Powerhouse / electrical shop
M. Fire station
N. Garage
O. Stores
P. Offices
Q. Main entrance
R. Heating station
S. Structural-steel drawing office
T. Pattern shop
U. Structural-steel templates

* High-speed launches

CONTENTS

PREFACE

There have been thousands of books written about airplanes, about their design, their operation, or about the people involved. Any number of anecdotes have been recounted, but it seems that few books have ever described the actual manufacture of aircraft.

This brief history of aircraft manufacture at Canadian Vickers, and its successor, Canadair, is a step toward redressing this omission.

The period covered is from 1923 to around 1984, so the Canadair Challenger is included, but not the later versions ~ the Regional Jets or the CL-415.

This work was prepared as an input to a larger volume issued for the 50th anniversary of Canadair Ltd. The present book covers the manufacturing aspects up to the end of the final line. Photographs have been selected to illustrate the early years.

The writer wishes to give thanks to Walter Allatt, Fred Hollylee, John McVicar, and Jim Moffatt, and authors Larry Milberry and Ron Pickler. He particularly wishes to acknowledge Ross Richardson and the late Hank Volker for access to their fine book and photo libraries.

Canadian Vickers and Canadair were both the type of company where, in some cases, the entire family was employed. My brother worked in the machine shop of Canadian Vickers in the 1940s. I worked for some 31 years at Canadair, from 1952 to 1984, and my son was a computer programmer at Canadair in the 1970s.

PHOTOGRAPHS

FOREWORD

I was very pleased when the publisher of Patrick Campbell's new book, *At the End of the Final Line*, approached me with a request to write the foreword to this volume. Canadian Vickers and Canadair are both well known to me, as they are to generations of Canadians, as great companies that provided employment to tens of thousands of workers over the years and produced aircraft that are respected the world over. I have been researching the history of Canadian Vickers for several years and am currently working on a corporate history that will emphasize the human side of such a large industrial organization.

My wife's grandfather, Tom Whitton, worked for Canadair for over 40 years, from the days of flying boats in Maisonneuve at the Canadian Vickers shipbuilding yard to the introduction of the Challenger in the late 1970s. My father, brother, and I all worked at the Canadian Vickers yard at various times from the 1950s to the late 1970s, so my interest in Patrick Campbell's new work is only natural.

Canadian Vickers in the early days was a subsidiary of the world's largest armaments company, Vickers Ltd. of Britain, and was able to draw upon the expertise of its trained shipwrights, carpenters and metal workers from the shipyard to assemble flying boats at the yard. The uncertainty of government support and lack of general industrial infrastructure in Canada at the time meant that companies such as Canadian Vickers had to become 'jacks of all trades', and become largely self-sufficient.

In modern parlance, this would be called a center of excellence in innovation. To the hard-working employees and managers of Canadian Vickers and Canadair, they were just trying to get the job done using any means at hand and the skills and acquired knowledge of their staff.

Their accomplishments were and remain remarkable. From a corner of the shipyard where yard workers assembled a few flying boats in 1920, to the present day where Canadair's new corporate identity of Bombardier is the world's third largest aircraft manufacturer, the development of this industry is due to the workmanship and ingenuity of its workers.

Patrick has decided to address a glaring omission in the literature of Canadian aviation history in describing the technology and processes used to manufacture aircraft from the early wood and fabric aircraft of the 1920s, up to the technology of the 1980s where aluminum and advanced metals, plastics, and composites are used.

Patrick has over 60 years experience in the building of aircraft in Britain and Canada, and remains active today in the Canadian Aviation Historical Society and the Canadian Aviation Heritage Centre, where aircraft that had a significant impact on Canadian aviation history are being re-built, and in some cases built from scratch according to the original blueprints.

I believe he is uniquely qualified to write the story of the manufacturing history of aircraft at Canadian Vickers and Canadair and hope that this book serves to inspire a new generation with its examples of world-class Canadian ingenuity, skills and workmanship

Jack Anderson
April 2006

12

There is a legend that the islands of Japan sprang, fully formed, from the eye of a goddess. This may have worked for Japan, but it just doesn't happen that way in the aircraft industry.

Almost all aircraft companies are the result of thousands of people working over a period of many years, of buildings and equipment, of financial investment, and perhaps most of all, of skills and technology.

The history of Canadian Vickers and Canadair is a very good example of this process, and this book will seek to review the history and development of those parts of the background of the company that are directly or indirectly involved in the manufacturing side of the business.

There can be no doubt that the historic roots of Canadair are found in the Canadian Vickers shipyard, a subsidiary of Vickers Ltd. of Great Britain. In 1912, the yard had been established in the city of Maisonneuve, at the foot of Viau Street, so that Canada could produce naval ships. In 1916, with shipbuilding under way, there came a demand for a Canadian source of aircraft engines, but that came to nothing. The idea was not, however, quite dead and the company turned to aircraft rather than engines. The first actual involvement came in 1920 when aircraft were needed for a trans-Canada flight, and the facilities of Canadian Vickers were chosen to assemble two huge Felixstowe F3 flying boats and a Fairey F-IIIC 'Transatlantic' seaplane on floats. For such work, a shipyard would have ample space, cranes to lift the parts, and ship fitters and riggers who had all the necessary skills (given some technical guidance) to do the assembly and lower the machines onto the waters of the St. Lawrence River, which was sheltered by a breakwater at the foot of the slipway (Fig.1).

This, of course, brings us to the first major consideration for Canadian Vickers: it was a shipyard, with no adjacent land from which land-based aircraft could be flown. There was also the further problem that the St. Lawrence was frozen, or the surface cluttered with ice, for a good deal of the year.

Because of this situation, most of the aircraft produced by Canadian Vickers were, of necessity, water-based ~ either flying boats or aircraft equipped with floats ~ although some of these could be fitted with skis or with wheels when occasion demanded.

Before we start discussing aircraft manufacturing, let us go back another 20 years to 17 December 1903. On this day Orville, and later, Wilbur Wright became the first men to achieve controlled flight under power. Others had flown before in balloons, kites, dirigibles, and gliders and had even lifted off the ground momentarily under power, but not under control. Theirs, then, can be considered the first successful heavier-than-air machine to achieve sustained powered flight, so it can be considered the starting point of our aviation industry.

Now, the construction of these early airplanes was aimed at achieving the lowest possible weight, for the power plants were only marginally sufficient to get the machine into the air. Such weight savings had been the target of two industries, the carriage builders and the bicycle builders. The Wrights had been in the latter trade, so they were able to design and build very light structures using wire-braced wooden frames, a few metal fittings and the lightest available fabrics to cover the whole structure. The technology was, therefore, established, and their methodical research led to their success. Construction required no special buildings and little machinery was required. Simple hand tools, band saws and circular saws, a simple lathe, and a rudimentary metal-working shop were sufficient to make all the parts.

This basic construction technique was to last for many years, continually being refined and improved, until the First World War caused a tremendous demand for aircraft. Large factories were built and large numbers of workers, men and women, were brought into the industry and trained. While some more advanced construction methods were developed, particularly in Germany, the vast bulk of the military aircraft, trainers, fighters, and bombers, continued to be made as wire-braced wooden structures, covered in fabric.

In 1923 Canadian Vickers began manufacture of their first aircraft ~ six Vickers 'Viking IV' flying boats (Fig. 2). They employed the same basic construction, followed by the very successful Canadian Vickers 'Vedette' flying boat (Figs. 3-8). The designer, W.T. Reid, had been brought over from Britain. Such manufacture required no particular new machinery or facilities. The skilled fitters of the shipyard were able to produce all the detail parts and continue with the assembly without major difficulties.

Once assembled, however, there came the problem of rigging. The fuselage structure would be set up, levelled, and fixed firmly in position. The central space-frame would then be carefully aligned by tightening and loosening the wire bracing by the use of turnbuckles. With the central space-frame aligned, the same method would be used to work outwards until the whole fuselage was correctly aligned; then the same methods would be used to set up the empennage and the wing structure. This type of work was, of course, not unfamiliar to former sailors working in the shipyard, and they would also be adept in the necessary splicing of all the cables used in the bracing system.

Finally, all the control surfaces would be installed and their limits of movement set by rigging boards to give the correct control surface movement when the control column and the rudder bars were actuated.

The engine installation, the adjustment of the thrust line, and the installation and proving of the various systems, fuel and oil, would follow. Then the final balancing was done to establish the location of the centre of gravity.

Those procedures, plus a compass swing, were the necessary prelude to ground runs, taxiing and the all-important first flight.

This, then, was the way that Canadian Vickers became established as one of Canada's early aircraft manufacturers.

Over the next years, Canadian Vickers continued producing the Vedettes, but also started work on design and construction of several other aircraft ~ flying boats, Varuna and Vista (Figs. 9, 10, 11), or float planes, Vanessa and Velos (Fig. 12). All of these were flown with various degrees of success, but in most cases only a prototype was built before the design was abandoned, the exception was the Varuna, a more successful private venture machine, of which eight were produced.

During this period, the Vigil was the only machine that was not water-borne. It was intended as a communications aircraft and was fitted with a wheeled undercarriage or skis. Again, there was no further production.

Simultaneously with the above, Canadian Vickers undertook the manufacture of three HS-3L flying boats, a license-built version of the Curtiss HS-2L with added wing bays.

The construction of these aircraft was essentially of wood, with some exceptions that will be discussed later. Aircraft of this type, particularly the flying boats, were ideal for the skills of a shipyard.

There was always a large lofting floor where the basic sections could be laid out full scale, using the old shipbuilding terms: offsets, waterlines and buttock lines. Similarly, the various parts of the airframe inherited the nautical nomenclature of ribs, bulkheads, keels, and stringers. The terms port, starboard, forward, aft, and athwartships were used and generally still are, to this day.

While on this theme, I will say that many of the earliest aircraft constructors were located in France, and it was there the Wright brothers went when their claim to be the first to fly was rejected in the United States. From the French we have inherited the terms *aileron, nacelle, empennage, fuselage, longeron,* and others. This is what happens when you start a new industry: words are needed to describe the parts and the processes, so the workers and the technologists borrow terms from their own background or take words that conveniently describe what they wish to identify.

We, therefore, see Canadian Vickers constructing wood, wire and fabric aircraft, developing skills as they went ~ all this just 20 years after the Wright brothers' historic event. It must be understood that, as Canadian Vickers was a shipyard, its greatest skills were in metalworking, but there was a marine joiners' shop for woodworking, so it was there that the parts for the essentially all-wood Viking IVs were built. A separate shop was set up for metal parts in the upper floor of the electrical maintenance shop, and machined parts were obtained from the marine machine shop. A drawing office was set up above the boiler room, and, of course, common use was made of general facilities such as First Aid, Timekeeping and Accounting.

In these early days, the Viking IV featured American elm for longitudinal members and spruce for transverse frames. The hull was planked with two-ply mahogany stitched together with copper wire. The HS-3L flying boat's hull consisted of pine or cedar planks, separated by glued fabric. Frames, keel and sternpost were of ash; the stringers and floor were pine or cedar. Bulkheads were three-ply waterproofed veneer, and engine-bearers were laminated in ash or spruce. The wings were supported by spruce spars, pine ribs and oval steel tube for the trailing edge. All surfaces were fabric covered with two coats of cellulose acetate dope, then two to four coats of cellulose nitrate, and finally one or two coats of grey enamel.

Every piece of wood, carefully chosen for its grain, was well seasoned or kiln dried. One of the greatest problems was the tendency of wood to become saturated over a period of time, and it was said that a Vedette hull could absorb some 300 pounds of water, a penalty charged directly against the payload.

From 1925 to 1928, Canadian Vickers manufactured 13 of the Avro 504N trainers (Figs. 13-14) under license from Avro in England, and 14 of the Avro 552 (Fig. 15), also on floats. These were really the last of the all-wood machines to be built; in some of the early machines wood was slowly being replaced with metal. The Vedettes had used steel tube structures in the empennage, and the last Vedette to be built ~ the Vedette VI ~ had an all-metal hull, although only one was built, in 1930. The Varuna flying boats had steel tube spars in the centre-section and in the lower wing stubs. The Vanessa was the first Canadian Vickers type with the fuselage and tail all fabricated from steel tube, although the wings were of wood, and all surfaces were fabric covered.

The Vista ~ a tiny monoplane flying boat with a 60-horsepower Genet engine ~ weighed in at only 655 pounds empty, with the hull all made out of duralumin sheet and steel tube for the empennage.

The Velos again featured welded steel tube for the fuselage and empennage, as well as for the lower wing spars. It featured welded steel ribs and the forward portion of the wing in corrugated aluminum. The upper wing was still in wood, fabric covered. In this way, metal construction gradually replaced wood, with some problems, but dramatic weight saving.

In 1928, work was begun on a total of 11 license-built Fairchild FC-2s (Fig. 16), also on the Velos and the Super Universal ~ real work-horse aircraft, well-suited to the Canadian climate. These, together with similar aircraft brought in from the US, operated on wheels, floats and skis very effectively. The FC-2s were again built with welded steel tube for fuselage and empennage, with fabric-covered wings of wood.

In 1928, Canadian Vickers proposed a new flying boat ~ the Vancouver (Fig. 17) ~ to replace the Varuna for forestry work. The Vancouver was to have a hull of Alclad aluminum, so it could operate off salt water, although it still had wooden wings, fabric covered. It proved reasonably satisfactory and was used in several roles; a total of six were built. A passenger version and a conversion for military use did not gain acceptance, but the Vancouver stayed in operation until 1939.

In the following years, Canadian Vickers produced license-built versions of the legendary Fokker Super Universals (Fig. 18) and the Bellanca Pacemaker. These used the familiar welded tube fuselage and wooden wings, but the Super Universal wing was something new, at least to Canadian Vickers. It was a cantilever wing, that is, a wing with no bracing struts, and the whole wooden structure was covered with plywood instead of the usual fabric.

The last of these wood, metal and fabric aircraft to concern Canadian Vickers was the Buhl CA-6, which was being built at Sault Ste-Marie for the Ontario Provincial Air Service. In this case, however, Canadian Vickers was only involved in some of the engineering work, and in the design and supply of the floats. The Buhl project was active during the years 1935 to 1937, and slightly overlapped the next major technology change for Canadian Vickers ~ the manufacture of all-metal aircraft. This change would, of course, require new skills, new technology and new machinery. The basic woodworking facilities, the fabric-covering shops and the small machine shop were to be replaced, and the workers either made redundant or retrained. Some of the woodworkers and some of the fabric-shop workers could be kept on to supply furnishings and upholstery, but 1936 was to be a watershed from which there would be no turning back.

This, then was the classic period that began in August 1920 when the trans-Canada aircraft were brought into the plant for assembly,. It ended in 1932, when the Great Depression reduced the total employment of the aircraft division of Canadian Vickers to just eight people, including R.J. 'Dick' Moffett, Aircraft Manager; Douglas A. Newey in Engineering and the Chief Inspector, C.J. Ferguson.

Before we leave this period, however, there is one matter of great significance that must be addressed. While we have discussed the building of the aircraft and the materials of construction, we have ignored the matter of tooling.

Aircraft construction is a compendium of conflicting requirements. The structure must be strong, yet light; it must also be rigid enough to carry the heavy loads of landing and take-off and the loads imposed on the airframe during manoeuvring. Flight in bad weather, especially near thunderstorms, can impose huge short-term loads, some of which will be imposed asymmetrically. For this reason, the airframe must also have a degree of flexibility, so that it bends before it breaks. The wing tips of some modern aircraft can be flexed up to 15 feet upwards or downwards, without failure, on structural test.

This mixture of rigidity and flexibility was achieved by the wire-and-strut-braced structures on both fuselage and wings of the classic aircraft. This requirement, together with the need to achieve a low weight, meant that the whole structure had to be essentially symmetrical. To achieve this, the basic fuselage structure had to be built on assembly jigs, then adjusted to final symmetry by rigging, as described above. The wings ~ with their load-bearing structure of spars, and the wing section ~ determined by the shape of the ribs, had to ensure that the shape of the port wing was identical to the shape of the starboard wing. Any discrepancy would mean that one wing would supply more lift or more drag than the other, and the resulting difference would have to be corrected by moving the control surfaces to achieve straight-line flight, with a consequent increase in drag, and loss of performance or payload.

In order to make the wing section symmetrical, every rib in the port wing would have to be identical in shape to that in the starboard wing. This was achieved by taking a flat plate of a stable material, marking out the desired profile on it, and installing blocks around the periphery. The actual rib material would be formed into this tool, then glued or fastened together to make a finished detail part. In some cases, duplicate tools could be made from a master tool to increase the production rate.

Should the wing be tapered from root to tip, or if the thickness of the wing was progressively reduced span-wise, then, of course, no two ribs would be the same, and two sets or families of tools would be required, one set for the port wing, and one set, in mirror image, for the starboard wing. Other tools would be required for the spars as well as for the assembly of the wing. A similar set of tools would be needed for the elevators and the rudder details, and additional fixtures for the final assembly of the parts. The engine mounts and the undercarriage would require welding fixtures to achieve the same symmetry. Tools also were needed to make replacement parts should they be required.

This whole art of tooling was developed to a very high degree in the aircraft industry, and required a great number of specialist tool designers, tool planners, and complex and exhaustive tool proving programs to support the manufacturing process.

With what I have termed 'the classic period of construction' nearing an end, the Great Depression made itself felt throughout all of industry. Demand for civil aircraft fell abruptly, and even government orders were hard to come by. The layoffs resulted in the aircraft division's losing all but eight employees, as noted above.

Then, when things were at their worst, came an order, small but significant, for a completely new type of machine that would herald a bewildering expansion over the next few years. The new type of construction was the all-metal, stressed-skin cantilever-wing monoplane. The first project to be tackled was for a quantity of aircraft to serve with the RCAF as high-performance photographic machines. The aircraft selected was the Northrop Delta, to be modified slightly, and built under license (Figs. 19, 20, 21), with an initial three of the Mark I, followed later by 17 of the Mark II version.

Now, Canadian Vickers had, as related above, built up some experience with welded tube structures, and with metal spars and ribs. Both aluminum and steel had been used for structure, and both floats and the hulls of flying boats had been fashioned out of metal, but the technology for making a complete aircraft out of metal had to be learned virtually from scratch. There would also be a need to obtain appropriate machinery and to hire and train suitable workmen. There was also a technical problem of developing written procedures for processing the various alloys so that consistent quality could be achieved. There was also need for an extensive assessment of the necessary specifications of the materials after which, when the right material had been chosen, the Procurement Department, which had also to be brought together, would be able to start its work. There would be need for a metallurgical laboratory, establishment of standards, testing equipment to prove the materials and to confirm that the heat treatment and protective finishes to be used were good enough for meeting industry standards. All in all, a tremendous task to face.

When the Delta order was placed, total personnel rose from 8 to 53. It rose to 62 the next year, and to 246 in 1937. By 1939 the Great Depression was pushed into history. As war became imminent, the race was to rebuild the RCAF. Canadian Vickers employment rose to 450, and factory area for building aircraft rose from 125,000 square feet to 190,000 square feet, a figure that would be quadrupled within the next few years.

Because the Northrop Delta is a milestone in the company history, not for the numbers built, but for the technology achieved, it is perhaps worthwhile to describe this machine rather more fully. It must also be borne in mind that we are talking of a time just over 30 years from the Wright Brothers' first flight, and only 12 years after Canadian Vickers began aircraft construction.

To give some idea of the problems, Ed Forrest, in his all too brief memoirs, describes his early experience with duralumin sheet brought from Britain. The material arrived in 4-foot by 12-foot sheets, somewhat buckled. After some work flattening the 50 sheets, it was determined that it could be bent only across the grain, so all marking-out had to be done accordingly. To facilitate working, a few drops of oil were spread on the surface, heat was applied with a blowtorch until the oil turned dark brown, and the flat-pattern parts were then quenched in cold water to be ready for forming. The same method was used for softening rivets. By the time the Vancouver flying boat was being manufactured, a salt bath had been obtained for the rivets and smaller parts, but as it was unsatisfactory for sheet material, an electric furnace was obtained, which gave good service from 1928 to 1942. The forming of extruded sections was a problem until rolls were devised. These were some of the difficulties to be overcome before the detail parts of the Delta could be built, and of course there would be tooling problems to be solved, also. While flat pattern templates, trim templates and other basic tooling would be familiar, there was need to develop sub-assembly jigs and fixtures, and to fabricate the major fuselage and wing assembly jigs.

It is of interest to note that the Northrop Delta was designed to be made in an American factory with hydro-forming capability. No such machine was available at Canadian Vickers, so wooden tools were built, faced with steel, with the flanges beaten by hand.

One interesting job that literally dropped from the skies was a repair job on the airship R-100. The great airship had left Cardington in England on 29 July 1930, and reached Montreal on the night of the 31st. En route, it had encountered a violent storm over Trois Rivières, and lost a good deal of the fabric from the stabilizers and rudder. After the ship had docked at the splendid new mooring mast at St. Hubert, a team of fabric workers was called in from Canadian Vickers to do a repair job before the trip onwards to Ottawa.

Returning to the Delta, there were two rather unusual features of the design, ~ a brainchild of the renowned Jack Northrop. One was that the fuselage was built in two major parts, split along the horizontal plane. There was an upper portion and a lower portion, and the lower portion was built in a large assembly jig that included the wing centre-section and the two stub wings. The engine mount, a welded tubular structure, was then added to the assembly, which also included the undercarriage pickup points. The fuel tanks, fabricated separately, were then inserted into the stub wings.

The other rather unusual feature was the construction of the wing. Instead of the wing's being supported on one or two main spars, as was the usual practice, the design included a multi-cellular structure, with ribs running fore-and-aft, and no less than five structural webs running span-wise, plus extruded angles at each web, and span-wise stringers as well. This gave a relatively light and very stiff structure, in which all the tensile and compressive loads were carried at the surface, and the shear loads by the internal webs. The whole wing structure was in 24 ST Alclad alloy. The term Alclad, by the way, indicates a skin material that was a sandwich of strong but corrosion-sensitive aluminum alloy in the centre, with a thin layer of pure aluminum on the outside surfaces. The pure aluminum would oxidize, and no further corrosion would occur, protecting the load-carrying centre of the sandwich. Attachment of the outer wing to the stub wings was accomplished by a number of bolts, rather than the few bolts used to attach the wings of an aircraft with conventional main spars. This design is also found on the famous Douglas DC-3 and on other Douglas military types, all originating with Northrop.

This multi-cellular wing, together with the *monocoque* (another French term) *fuselage*, had the great advantage of offering internal spaces that were not cluttered up and criss-crossed with bracing wires, as was found in the classic construction, so it was much easier to install equipment and systems.

The Delta, once assembled, was given a protective coat of red oxide, and then the whole exterior was painted with finely ground aluminum powder, mixed with a clear lacquer, to give the 'silver' finish on which to apply the appropriate markings and identification.

The first flight of the prototype was on 16 August 1936, followed by delivery to the RCAF on September 1st. Production difficulties must have been well in hand, for the second aircraft was delivered on 17 October and the third on 31 October.

Before we move forward to the next challenge for Canadian Vickers, it might be interesting to look at another aspect. If we examine the empty weight of the various aircraft ‒ the weight of the aircraft as constructed, before the addition of crew, passengers, fuel, and payload ‒ we find that most of the aircraft weighed in at from 2,000 to 4,000 pounds. The only exceptions were the tiny Vista (655 pounds), and the larger machines ‒ the twin-engine Varuna, Velos

and Vancouver ~ and the single-engine HS-3L flying boat. The Northrop Delta had an empty weight of 4,600 pounds, so it was a familiar size to Canadian Vickers.

The next project, licensed production of the Supermarine Stranraer (Figs 22, 23, 24), involved a flying boat almost three times the size of the Delta, and over twice the size of the Velos or the Vancouver. The Stranraer was for coastal patrol. In November 1936 the RCAF ordered three, a number that was successively increased until 40 had been delivered.

Apart from the size, the construction was within Canadian Vickers' capability. The hull was of Alclad sheet, the wings and empennage structure were of duralumin and all surfaces were fabric covered. There were many stainless steel fittings, chosen for suitability in the corrosive sea-water environment. Interplane struts were also stainless. The sea-water environment also required that the aluminum parts were to be anodized, which was new to Canadian

Vickers, so they built their own tanks for the processing. The Stranraer used the Bristol Pegasus engines, with a total power of 1600 HP ~ over twice that of any previous machine built by Canadian Vickers ~ but the engines and the airframe gave good service. Many of these aircraft survived the war to go into civilian service.

It is interesting to see that Canadian Vickers, with its marine experience, built the Stranraer just as they would build the hull of a ship. The keel was laid down first, then the frames erected, followed by attachment of the keelsons, the intercostals and the stringers. The hull was plated and all joints sealed with white and black Bostik compound, then filled with water to check for leaks ~ simple and effective. One rather curious procedure was the practice of naming the continuous longitudinal members 'intercostals'; the shorter members, interrupted at each frame, were termed 'stringers'. This is the opposite of normal ship-building nomenclature, or that of most land-based aircraft.

The wing construction started in the spar shop, which was upstairs in Shop 8, where the internally corrugated spars, with heavy channels top and bottom, were built. Flat and tubular ribs were added and all the various attachment points built in. The spars were taken downstairs to the wing-assembly shop, then finally to the fabric shop where workers, mainly women, sewed on the Irish linen covering. After this, all surfaces were sprayed in the dope room with an acetone-based finish. Nacelles, struts and wing tip floats, as well as all the tail surfaces, were fabricated in the upstairs shop and fed to the assembly shop.

Canadian Vickers also made the propellers ~ ten laminations of Honduras mahogany, covered with fabric and a brass leading edge, and the whole encased in a hard celluloid mantle. The first Stranraer delivered was accepted on the understanding that the price did not include the propellers because they did not give the promised performance. They were therefore 'borrowed' so the prototype could be flown to Dartmouth before the St. Lawrence River froze. There was now room for assembly of the second machine.

The Stranraers served the RCAF well on both the Pacific and Atlantic coasts until they were all replaced in service by the more modern Consolidated Canso flying boats in 1944. Experience gained on the all-metal Delta and the much larger Stranraer was to prove invaluable to Canadian Vickers, and allowed the company to move forward into its two major wartime projects.

The first of these was the licensed production of major parts of the Handley-Page Hampden bomber. Chosen as a wartime program to help Britain, several Canadian companies were formed into a consortium to produce some 160 Hampdens. Canadian Vickers set up an assembly line in Shop 5, which was located north of the railway and south of Notre Dame Street, just west of the drawing office.

A total of 80 complete fuselages were produced in this shop for Canadian Associated Aircraft and, being land-aircraft, were delivered to the Canadian Consolidated Aircraft, Ltd. at St. Hubert for assembly, flight test, and subsequent delivery to Britain. While this program raised the capability and confidence of Canadian Vickers, it was in no way as significant as the next challenge -- the commencement in 1942 of the last and the biggest of all the aircraft programs to be tackled by the company.

With the outbreak of war, the need to replace the Stranraer biplane for maritime patrol and search-and-rescue was obvious, and the selected successors were the Consolidated PBY flying boat and the PBY-5A amphibian. Orders were placed with Boeing of Canada in Vancouver and Canadian Vickers in Montreal. Now, as the Stranraer was much larger than the Delta, the PBY-5A was, at an empty weight of nearly 25,000 pounds, double the size of the Stranraer. As well, it required an increase in production rate from the Stranraer's peak of four a month at the end of 1941, to a rate of 30 a month in June 1944 for the PBY-5A.

Over the period January 1943 to November 1944, Canadian Vickers delivered 312 PBY-5A amphibians (Figs. 25, 26), which included 139 of the Canso A version for the RCAF, and 173 of the OA-10A version for the U.S. Navy. The first 30 had been assembled from Canadian Vickers parts, and assembled and test-flown from the Canadian Consolidated Aircraft Ltd. plant at St. Hubert, while the balance of 282 were assembled and test flown from the new Vickers plant at Cartierville (see p. 30). This plant was then taken over by the new Crown company, Canadair Ltd., on 11 November 1944, and a further 57 of the OA-10A versions were produced for a total of 369 machines. Strangely enough, all the Canadair-built machines went to the U.S., and none to the RCAF.

Apart from its much greater size, the PBY-5A had a slightly more advanced type of construction. The higher rate of production required much more sophisticated basic tooling, as well as duplicate or rate tooling. Many additional tools and machines were required to replace the manually produced parts of the Stranraer. There was a need to expand the work force from 1,100 to 9,000 and to more than triple the floor space available.

The same Shop 8 at Canadian Vickers, sometime called the Maisonneuve Shop, was again used for manufacturing of the hull, which was, unlike the Stranraer, built in an inverted position, keel uppermost. The basic frames or bulkheads were made up as sub-assemblies, then brought to the assembly positions. The two first frames, which ran from the keel up to the wing pick-up points, had to be assembled in a pit in the floor as a centre-hull sub-assembly, then brought into the first of the two main hull assembly jigs where the rest of the frames were put in place, followed by keelsons, intercostals and stringers. Finally, separate 'plating' or 'skinning' crews, each consisting of a riveter and a bucker, completed the hull. The completed hull structures were then taken out of the assembly jigs, turned over (keel now down) to one of four floor positions. Here other crews would install lockers, stowage, controls, equipment, and wiring. One other crew would go over all hull joints, sealing them with zinc chromate tape. There was one further floor position where the hull could be filled with water up to floor level to check for leaks.

One new construction feature of the big amphibian was the 'wet wing' or integral fuel tanks. Between the two main wing spars, the entire volume of the centre section of a wing was filled with 1,458 litres (1,750 US gallons) of fuel in two large tanks, port and starboard. This gave a 750-pound weight-saving, and meant more fuel could be carried for a longer range. The sealing of the tanks had to be mastered, as

this was quite new to Canadian Vickers. Some U.S.-built machines incorporated a self-sealing liner in the tanks, but not the versions produced at St. Hubert and Cartierville. Perhaps the greatest lessons to be learned, however, were the problems of producing relatively large airplanes in quantity at a rate of up to 30 per month.

The first 30 were produced at St. Hubert, as the Maisonneuve facilty was running out of space. That was when the Canadian government decided to build a new plant next to the Cartierville Airport in St.Laurent, starting in December 1942. The Vickers shipyard would lose its aircraft construction, but would continue building ships. During WWII they would build over 300 ships and a few submarines. By July 1943, the transfer of Candian Vickers was complete and the first PBY-5A was ready for delivery from Cartierville in September of the same year. The change of name from Canadian Vickers to Canadair Ltd. (exclusively aircraft,

no ships) on 11 November 1944, had little effect on production, which continued until the last OA-10A rolled off the line in early 1945. The Canadair plant, in addition to the delivery of complete aircraft, had also produced some 119 hulls, 172 centre-sections and numerous PBY wingtip floats for U.S. suppliers. (Figs. 27A, 27B)

Now came a critical time for the company, for the cessation of World War II clearly meant an end to military production. In a series of astute moves, Benjamin Franklin, the president, obtained a contract from the Canadian Government to manufacture a civilian airliner for Trans-Canada Airlines, setting up a new line of work that would keep the production-line employees working while the design and tooling of the new airliner proceeded.

This new line of work was based upon the purchase of the entire work in progress of the Douglas factory at Oklahoma City, which had been producing the DC-3/C-47 aircraft. Also purchased were the parts and tooling of the Pullman works in Chicago, which had been producing C-47 wings. Of equal value, the C-54 plant at Parkridge, Illinois, was also purchased. As a result, some 600 carloads of machines, tools and material were soon on their way to Cartierville, purchased at a cost of $40 per ton for tooling, and $200 per ton for aircraft parts. The U.S. plants had, of course, been closed down as contracts were cancelled, so the material was deemed little above scrap value.

The trainloads of parts were brought by rail into the Noorduyn plant on Bois Franc Road, which had a spur line into the factory. A lucrative business was soon underway, as the world airlines clamoured for DC-3 aircraft, spare parts, and conversions for civil use. In 1945, some 16 conversions and repairs were made, 104 in 1946, and a fairly steady flow continued through to 1950.

While this work had not brought any significant new technology to the company, it had kept the production personnel well occupied and made the company viable. This led, in time, to the outright buyout of the firm by Electric Boat. The name Canadair Ltd. remained, and the amalgamation later became General Dynamics. Many more companies were later added to the group, including Convair, one of whose parents had been Consolidated, designer of the PBY (Consolidated Model 28) series of aircraft.

The other and even more important move was the landing of the contract to provide a modern airliner, with transatlantic capability, for Trans-Canada Airlines.

The chosen airframe was that of the C-54, which was a military version of the DC-4, but it was agreed to install Rolls-Royce Merlin engines in demountable power plants. This was a particularly happy choice for Canadair, as the material purchased in the U.S. provided fuselages, finished and semi-finished parts, sub-assemblies, tooling, and sample parts.

While the shops worked on the conversion of military C-47 and C-53 aircraft to the civil DC-3 configuration, with much help from Douglas, and much consultation with Trans-Canada, Canadair engineering got on with the redesign because, apart from the installation of the Merlin engines, the Trans-Canada machines had to be pressurized, which was a first for Canadair. To speed up matters, the first machines off the line were to be unpressurized, and would include a large proportion of the parts and assemblies brought up from the U.S. These were designated DC-4M-1 (Fig. 27c) to distinguish them from the American aircraft. The empty weight was to be more than double that of the PBY-5A/OA-10A and the design included a somewhat more complex 'wet-wing'.

Planning and tool-making proceeded rapidly, and a proper production line was set up in the high-bay of Building 102. The new airplane, now known as the North Star, first flew on 14 July 1946 with its CF-TEN-X registration, and was followed by other versions for the RCAF, Trans-Canada Airlines, CPA and BOAC, who changed the name of their machines to Argonaut (Fig. 28).

As the second post-war civil transport after the Constellation, the North Star series kept the Canadair manufacturing capabilities very busy from 1946 until 1950, when the last machine came off the line. Another important benefit of this program was that a large local workforce became trained and available. Plus, an aggressive hiring action brought in a flow of skilled personnel from Britain, Holland, Germany, Poland, and elsewhere, for most other aircraft companies were reducing rather than increasing staff.

As this was the first pressurized aircraft built at Canadair, it is interesting to see the need to face up to the very serious problems encountered with the pressurization system. There had been no such system on the C-54 or the DC-4 aircraft, so it was all new and the final satisfactory solution took all the resources of Canadair, Trans-Canada, Rolls-Royce, and Godfrey Engineering. The technical expertise of a company is based upon the ability to recognize and solve such problems, normally avoided when simply building aircraft under license.

Before we go on to Canadair's next momentous step, perhaps it would be well to discuss one very important topic we have touched upon very lightly up to now. There is an ancient saying that you cannot make bricks without straw, and it is equally true that you cannot build airplanes without tooling. A great deal has always been said about the design and flying of aircraft, much less about their manufacture and virtually nothing about the tool planning, the tool fabrication, and the process planning that turn a design concept into an aircraft that can be rolled out for its inaugural flight.

It is therefore worthwhile to make a further study of this subject ~ a brief study, but a vital link in a chain of events we are following.

The earliest of all the techniques of tooling came from the shipbuilding industry. The practice was to build a model or a half-model of the hull. Its design would provide room for cargo, volume enough for floatation, and fairing of the lines of the bow and stern to meet the demands of the sea. It was necessary that lines should meet practical considerations of curvature, whether the vessel was to be skinned with wooden planks or steel plates.

With the basic shape established, the main cross-sections, or offsets, would be laid out, full scale, on a 'lofting' floor (Fig. 29). The ribs and bulkheads were produced for subsequent erection onto the keel ~ on the stocks for ships, or in the fuselage assembly fixture for aircraft. This was how all the Canadian Vickers flying boats were developed, and there was still a lofting floor in use at Canadair well into the 1960s. It was mainly for the design of fuselages, nacelles, and the portions of the structure where the

wings and empennage surfaces faired into the fuselage or nacelle.

This process was made much simpler, and more accurate, when the huge Robertson camera came into use. This could photograph the lines onto sheets of aluminum up to 12 feet long, with astonishing accuracy. Workers would then cut and file to the lines, preparing full-scale templates that represented the exterior shape of the aircraft to the inner mould line of the skin.

The next step would be to erect these cross-sections on a base, secure them in their correct stations with nuts and threaded rods, then to cover the whole assembly ~ a particular part of the airplane - with plaster, known as a Plaster-master (Fig. 30), which represented a particular part of the airplane. On the surface would be scribed the lines where frame, bulkheads,longerons, and stringers would be placed.

After consultation between the tool-planning people and the process planners, a decision would be made as to which machine in the plant would produce the parts most economically and efficiently, and the appropriate tools would then be made. In some cases, this would be done by taking a plaster 'splash' directly off the Plaster-master, and then, in the foundry, making a sand mould, from which a die would be made that would be an exact copy of the Plaster-master. In 1949, Canadair purchased an interesting machine to assist in making tools; the machine was known as the Keller (Fig. 31), named after Helen Keller (1880-1968) who lost her sight and hearing before she was two years old, and had to use her sense of touch to learn to write and to speak. This machine traced the contours of a model, mounted on its upper table, with a stylus, and reproduced it, three-dimensionally, from a metal block mounted on a lower table. This process became known as 'kellering'. The die, usually made of kirksite, would then be placed on a press, oiled, and the parts made. Sometimes these would be placed on a hydraulic press, a stretch press, or, for some deeper draws, a double-acting press. In some cases a lead punch would be cast off the kirksite die, and the two conforming tools be placed in a drop hammer. The sheet metal, usually in a soft, or annealed, condition, would be pressed or hammered into shape, and later trimmed in another tool, drilled in yet another, and finally heat-treated to achieve the full material properties before anodizing or painting.

This is but one simple example of the type of expertise that had to go into one single part, and there were, for example, thousands of different parts required for the completed manufacture of an airframe.

In addition, there would be the requirement for assembly jigs for all sub-assemblies, for the major assemblies, and finally major assembly jigs for producing the larger assemblies that would feed the final line.

All this is a far cry from the early days when metal parts were formed by hand. Skins had been hand-wheeled, one at a time, and checked on a wooden 'egg-crate', in order to achieve the correct contour, before being attached to the airframe structure. Quantity production, such as the 56 aircraft per month coming off the final line at Canadair in 1953, would have been utterly impossible without sophisticated tooling even if there had been a work-force with the skills to make aircraft one at a time.

In time, of course, the whole art of tooling changed with the advent of 5-axis machining, and tools could be cut to the complex shapes required without going through the above process, but there still remained the need for all the special trim jigs, drill jigs, milling fixtures, assembly jigs and fixtures, as well as the necessary handling fixtures and special tools without which the production line would be impossible.

The above is only the barest outline, but it may give some idea of the problems to be solved, and the skills that had to be developed.

Mention has been made of Canadair's next momentous step ~ the manufacture of a total of 1,815 fighter aircraft, initially based upon the North American F-86A and F-86E, known in Canada as the Sabre 1, Sabre 2 and Sabre 4. These were followed by a version with the Orenda engine from Avro Canada, and identified as the Sabre 3, Sabre 5 and Sabre 6. (Figs. 32, 33, 34)

Now, up to this point, Canadair had developed some skill in producing what we can refer to as 'sheet metal' aircraft, for most of the parts were cut and formed from sheet aluminum, skinned with the same and held in place with aluminum rivets. Production had been done on relatively simple tooling by a fairly skilled workforce. Because the structure was predominately made from sheet metal, the machinery, or capital equipment, was not very extensive, nor especially sophisticated: some conventional lathes, drilling and milling machines, a few grinders, a mechanical press, a couple of hydroforming presses, a stretch press, and the usual shears, brake presses, hand-wheeling machines, and planishing hammers.

With the advent of the Sabre, Canadair was to experience a considerable step forward in technology, and, at the same time, a very large number of complex aircraft was to be produced to a very demanding schedule.

The first problem was that North American Aviation would be keeping the U.S. version, the F-86E, in simultaneous production, so Canadair could not take over the tooling. The high production rate, initially set at 10 at month, but later to rise to 20 a month, and to peak at 50 a month, required a moving assembly line, more like those found in the automobile industry than in aircraft manufacture. There would also be a need for extensive duplicate tooling and sub-contract work that would involve coordination problems that would, in turn, necessitate master tools, rate tooling and coordination tools.

The problem of having a large number of aircraft available on short notice necessitated interchangeability of parts so spare parts could be inserted by Air Force personnel when damage occurred. Now, the structure of the Sabre was once described as 'the ultimate in conventional design,' which is apt, as the airframe was largely made up of parts formed from aluminum sheet and plate, with a variety of rolled sections and extrusions. There was also a good deal of stainless steel used in the structure, due to the high temperatures around the tailpipe.

One main structural feature was the massive intake duct (Fig. 35), which required no bifurcation or boundary-layer bleeds, but ran directly from the inlet back to the engine bay. This was constructed as a single unit, and formed the backbone of the whole aircraft structure. This sub-assembly carried the pressurized cockpit, as well as pick-up points for the wing centre section and the after fuselage.

35

The wing, with a 35° sweep-back at 25% chord, was made in five parts ~ centre-section, outer panels and wing tips ~ but, because the wing housed self-sealing fuel tanks, the centre-section and inner portions of the wing had a double-skin structure, with some of the riveting done with explosive rivets. The aircraft also introduced Canadair to 'coin-dimpling' of skins to achieve flash riveting in certain areas. The most significant feature of all was that virtually all the wing skins had to be machined from 75 ST aluminum plate, as the skins tapered in the span-wise direction. This had to be done on large skin-mills, but the result was a very robust wing structure that was bolted together as a single entity, complete with the main undercarriage, and offered up for assembly on the final line as a single unit. The wing of the earlier aircraft also incorporated full-span leading edge slats, power operated ailerons, and inboard flaps. There was also a requirement to 'shave' the rivets flush in the aerodynamically critical areas of wing, fuselage and tail to preserve the boundary layer as far aft as possible.

While the rear fuselage and empennage appeared conventional, there were many new problems to be overcome in the complex control systems, but all were solved in time.

It should be added that, for the Sabre, the entire structure was designed to stand the stress of violent manoeuvre at high Mach-numbers, and even the forces encountered in a transsonic dive. Aerodynamic performance dictated that virtually all the external surfaces were formed of complex shapes, involving three-dimensionally curved surfaces, with the commensurate requirement for external skins to be pressed, drop-hammered, or stretch-pressed into the required shapes, and for the supporting structure to be formed or machined accordingly. All of that involved not only a tooling and planning problem, but it required a considerable capital expenditure in procurement and installation of new machinery, and the training of the necessary operators.

The first of these new machines was purchased in 1950. More drop-hammers, mechanical and hydro-forming presses, milling machines and stretch presses were followed in the next two years by yet more milling machines, mechanical presses, a large skin-milling machine, and a versatile hydro-forming press, the Verson. The great advantage of the Verson was that a number of different parts, each on its own relatively simple tool, could be made simultaneously and to great accuracy. In fact, because the tools had all been made for use on the normal hydro-forming press, which had to make allowance for material springback, most of the tools had to be remanufactured for the Verson process.

In addition to the structural challenges, the Sabre introduced Canadair to power-assisted controls, for the manoeuvre loads would impose control force requirements beyond the strength of the pilot. There were also some other features new to Canadair: the radar-gun sight systems, the 'flying-tail', and, later on, the changes to the airframe and the tooling to substitute a Canadian engine, the Orenda, for the American J-47 engine that had powered the Sabre 1, 2 and 4 versions.

Many U.S.-made parts were incorporated in the first aircraft off the line, but more and more Canadair-made parts were being used. Soon, some 85% of the aircraft was 'made in Canada' from raw material and purchased parts from Canadian sources.

Apart from its outstanding acceptance as a world-class fighter aircraft, happily seldom used in combat, the Canadian Sabre brought Canadair world acceptance as a manufacturer and brought the company's manufacturing capability ahead in a great leap forward. During this period, company employment jumped from 5,000 to 13,495 employees, but not entirely due to the Sabre production.

In those days, much of the workforce arrived at work by streetcar, riding from Montréal up to the Garland Terminus at Van Horne Avenue, then taking a car up to the Poirier stop for Plant 1, or taking a car that turned off the Cartierville line to run along Bois Franc to Plant 4 or Plant 2 ~ the end of the line (Fig. 36).

On Tuesday, 30 October 1951, their Royal Highnesses, Princess Elizabeth and the Duke of Edinburgh, were welcomed to Canadair by John Jay Hopkins, Chairman and President of Canadair and President of Electric Boat Company of New York (Fig. 37).

It may be noted that when the Princess and her husband, while visiting Kenya, were informed of the death of her father, George VI, they flew back to London in a Canadair Argonaut of BOAC. The Princess was now the Queen.

While the RCAF had a fine fighter in the Sabre, there was also a need for a two-seater aircraft to train the pilots for the Sabre. For this role, the aircraft selected was the Lockheed T-33, but it was to be modified somewhat to be powered by the Rolls-Royce Nene engine instead of the American J-33.

Preparations for manufacture began immediately following the start of work on the Sabre, and the two types were to remain in almost simultaneous production for the next eight years, until 656 of the trainers had come off the Canadair production line.

For the Canadair T-33 AN (Figs 38, 39), the N designated Nene, the engine, and for the prototype an X for experimental was added. It was otherwise virtually identical to the Lockheed-built T-33A trainer, which was itself a development of the Lockheed P-80 fighter, the first jet aircraft to enter squadron service with the U.S. Air Force. The P-80 first prototype had flown in January 1943, and the second in June 1944. Some were flown by the USAF in England and Italy before the end of the war, but none made it into combat. The T-33, being almost literally a two-seater version, therefore represented World War II construction, so it was a purely sheet-metal airplane. Production at Canadair, therefore, required no special machinery or new technology, which was just as well, for the Sabre structure was enough of a problem without additional challenges. The T-33 also had a straight, rather than a swept wing, and the Nene fitted well into the fuselage designed to take the GE I-40 or the J-33 engines, both of which used centrifugal flow compressors, so there was sufficient diameter to house the similar Nene engine.

Canadair had, however, to produce a complete set of tools, as the T-33 was still in production in the U.S. The Sabre production line was situated in the former Noorduyn plant on Bois Franc Road, known as Plant 2 by Canadair, so that left the production line for the T-33 to replace the North Star /Argonaut line in Plant 1. Most of the plant was used for the T-33, apart from the Sabre canopy and engine inlet duct that were produced in amongst the T-33 sub-assemblies. The near-conventional T-33 wing incorporated fully-machined tapered spars, which were milled in Plant 1, and a Drivematic automatic-riveting machine (Fig. 40) replaced a good deal of hand-bucked riveting.

One very nice feature was that the main fuselage, from the separate nose sub-assembly to the monocoque rear fuselage, was split into two halves. The split was on the vertical centre line, unlike the Northrop Delta that had been split in the horizontal plane. This meant that two halves of the T-33 fuselage, incorporating the cockpit and the engine bay, moved down the assembly line parallel to each other, but wide apart. All the equipment, wiring, piping and other systems could, therefore, be conveniently installed at waist level before the two halves joined further up the line. The nose would be

added, then the wing with the main under-carriage. Later the engine would be inserted, and, finally, the aft fuselage, with empennage attached, would be wheeled into place.

Another example of the more advanced design of the Sabre is that, on the T-33, the leading edges were attached by hundreds of machine screws and captive floating nuts. The Sabre leading edge featured a piano-type hinge on the upper and lower surfaces. Removal of the leading edge was by use of a rivet gun to drive the piano-wire pin that passed through the hinge or, similarly, the wire could be with-drawn, releasing the leading edge. This facili-tated maintenance and repairs.

The first flight of T-33 ANX, the proto-type, was on December 22, 1952, and the plant would soon build to a production rate of 1½ per day. Early on, wings, rear fuselage and the empennage were subcontracted, but, in time, all parts were produced in Canadair.

In 1953, a new record was achieved by Canadair, when a total of 4,572,000 pounds of aircraft, or over 2,200 tons, was produced in a single year. This consisted of 479 Sabres and 204 of the T-33 aircraft. This eclipsed the previous record of 3,352,000 pounds, which represented production of 228 Canso amphibians in 1944.

In 1952, Canadair became involved in a joint program with Beech of Wichita, to produce the T-36, a twin-engine 'hot rod', said to be a utility trainer/transport. However, it was promptly cancelled by the Eisenhower Administration when he came into power. Looking back, it looked like a business-jet, but was a bit premature. Canadair's task was to build the cabin from the flight deck aft, the rear fuselage, and some centre wing and other wing parts. Some of these would have been subcontracted, but Canadair built many detail parts and a good deal of tooling, as well as instrumenting the wing of the prototype with strain gauges and thermocouples. A special machine was procured to do automatic riveting on the wing leading edge, but the program was cut before the process had been successfully developed.

Another joint program, this time with de Havilland, involved the Grumman CSF-2 'Tracker' aircraft, with Canadair manufacturing 100 rear fuselages of conventional sheet metal construction, but including a large retractable radome. A full-size Plaster-master was made up, and a tool made in which the fibreglass radome was laid up, with a fibreglass honeycomb core. Even these smaller programs involved some new technology, or extension of existing practices.

Another interesting subcontract at this time was to install an Orenda PS -13 Iroquois engine on the rear fuselage of a Boeing B-47 as a flying test bed. (Figure 41) shows the dramatic arrival of the B-47, and (Figure 42) shows the same aircraft with the Iroquois engine in its nacelle.

The next major program for Canadair commenced in 1952, when the RCAF required a maritime patrol aircraft to replace the aging Avro Lancasters. The final selection was a much modified version of the Bristol Britannia air liner, but to be equipped with turbo compounded piston engines, and to be unpressurized. The reasons for the choice were that, by choosing an existing airplane, a great deal of aerodynamic and structural problems would be avoided.

The engines were chosen to achieve long-range and long-duration flights at low altitudes to enable surveillance of shipping and submarine activity. For the same reason, there was no need for the complexity and weight of a pressurization system. There was also the requirement for various holes in the structure of maritime patrol aircraft, out of which flares, sono-buoys, bombs, life rafts, etc., would be dropped, which would make pressurization difficult, although not impossible.

However, having said all that, the CL-28 Argus (Fig. 43) was, for Canadair, a relatively state-of-the-art design when it entered production in 1957. While the structure was more or less conventional, it should be noted that the empty weight of the CL-28 was approximately twice that of a North Star, or four times the empty weight of a Canso. On the other hand, the modest production rate, to peak at one a month in 1958, was not too demanding and there was no need for further expansion of the factory (Fig. 44).

Apart from a very large tooling program, which very conveniently followed the completion of the F-86 and T-33 tooling programs, there was the need to Americanize the entire structure to North American standards for American aluminium, American fasteners and American screw threads. There was no Canadian source for these products or for aircraft-quality sheet. There was also need for completely new systems to support the proposed role, and a complete full-scale fuselage mock-up to locate the crew and all the complex equipment. There was, because of the conventional structure, no great need for new capital equipment, although the recently-purchased Robertson camera greatly aided the tooling process. With this, the lines, formerly lofted by hand, could be transferred photographically onto sensitized aluminum sheets, and then cut and filed by hand to contour. This greatly expedited assembly of the metal structure for the Plaster-masters, and for establishing the flat-metal shape of parts on the raw material from which both tools and parts were made.

Other innovations for this program were the introduction of a new material, titanium, used in the form of flat sheet for the fire walls, and the use of a new steam-heated autoclave for metal-to-metal bonding, plus a clean-room where the parts could be laid-up before the bonding process. Another new feature was the introduction of optical tooling to align the major assembly tools. (Fig. 45)

While not directly involved in the manufacturing process, the CL-28 demanded many very complex and expensive test rigs to prove the various new systems to be developed. A major item was a rig to prove the new alternating current electrical system that supplied the demands of the radar systems, the Magnetic-Anomaly Detector (MAD), and even a large high-intensity searchlight that was installed in the wing.

The Mk.1 version also required a huge fibreglass and honeycomb radome to protect the search radar, so there was a challenge for both tooling and the bonding shops for this, and for the huge MAD boom of similar construction. In the same vein, one entire section of the structure of the vertical fin and rudder was made of non-conducting fibreglass, so the metal part of the surfaces above could be isolated from the airframe and serve as an antenna!

With the CL-28 program well in hand, Canadair started work on a cargo and passenger version for the RCAF, but there was another, short-lived program in between. This was to build a quantity of relatively short-range cargo/passenger transports for the RCAF. These were the CL-66 Cosmopolitans. Apart from the change from the basic Convair 340 and 440 design to accommodate the Napier Eland engine at first, the Cosmopolitan was, for Canadair, a relatively conventional sheet-metal airplane, and involved no new technology or capital equipment.

With the CL-28 still in production, as well as the CL-66, Canadair embarked on a new program involving planning and tooling work, mock-up and experimental work, yet still with no great capital expenditures on machinery.

This was the manufacture of the Canadair CL-44-6 transport (Fig. 46), to be known in the RCAF as the Yukon. This aircraft was a direct derivative of the CL-28, although it reverted to

much of the Britannia format, for it was a pressurized passenger aircraft with turbine engines. There was also a good deal of commonality with the CL-28, particularly the wing, tail surfaces and undercarriage. Much of the tooling, the stress calculations, and the aerodynamics had already been established. For the engines, Canadair selected the Rolls-Royce Tyne, a more powerful engine than the Bristol Proteus engines used on the British machine. The empty weight of the Bristol Britannia had been 82,500 pounds, and the CL-28 was 81,000 pounds, but the CL-44-6, when 'Americanized', stretched by 12 feet and strengthened for the cargo role, weighed in at some 91,000 pounds.

Another complication was that, since the experience gained on the pressurizing of the North Star series of aircraft, things were a lot more demanding after the disastrous fatigue failure of the de Havilland Comet aircraft in 1953/54. Under the latest airworthiness requirements, an entire CL-44 fuselage had to be proven in 'life-cycle' tests underwater, in a huge tank built at Plant 4. Here, brutal cuts were made in the fuselage, while under full pressure, to prove the structure to be 'fail-safe'. A total of 12 of these aircraft was produced over the years 1959-1961, and they served the RCAF well for many years.

Meanwhile, the company believed there was a place in the commercial market for a large capacity freight-carrying aircraft, so the CL-44/ Britannia airframe was modified by two significant manufacturing changes. The first was made because the FAA would not certify an aircraft for civil use with such poor forward vision for the pilots. From the pilot's seat, there were only about eight inches of forward vision between the top of the instrument panel and the lower side of the overhead panel ~ rather like the view a medieval knight would have had through his visor.

The new machine, to be designated CL-44D4 (Figs. 47, 48), required a tooling change to incorporate the much bigger windshield, and a test article to confirm the ability of the structure to withstand the impact of a large bird strike.

The second, and major change, was the incorporation of the swing-tail. This was the one-and-only case of swinging aside the entire rear section of a pressurized airliner, but the engineering and manufacturing problems were solved and the feature was entirely successful. Other solutions have been found, like the lifting 'visor' in the nose of the C-5A, or the clamshell doors in the nose of the Bristol Freighter. Various aircraft used an aft-ramp, particularly where air-drop or low-level cargo extraction was required, but the CL-44 D4 solution proved a very popular feature with the operators of the aircraft. Part of the problem had been the design and manufacture of the hinges that had to support the weight of the rear fuselage and empennage in a crosswind. Other problems had been the manufacture of the alignment and the locking mechanisms, the hydraulic actuation system, and the transfer of the controls to rudder and elevators that had to disconnect when the tail swung aside and reconnect upon closing. All these were solved.

The last major development of the type was the CL-44J, a modified form of the D4, with a 25-foot stretch and an empty weight of 114,315 pounds. This was the heaviest in Canadair history.

A space was selected in Building 117, and tooling was set up to support the airframe, with the support structure of the rear portion rolling on rails set in the floor, and the forward portion similarly supported. With the joints opened up, the nose section was rolled 10 feet ahead, and the tail 5 feet back, and a new structure inserted, with satisfactory results.

In 1958, after years of building other companies' designs, even if substantially modified, Canadair finally started design, tooling and manufacture of an entirely original design, the two-seat CL-41 trainer aircraft (Figs. 49, 50, 51). Of course, when a company is designing the structure from scratch, it stands to reason that it will seek a design that requires machinery and processes already in-house, so the final product was a conventional construction.

One unusual feature, for Canadair, was that the prototypes were built in a 'skunkworks', a system where designers, tool planners, production planners, material and process and quality personnel, together with procurement, are all located together on a particular area of shop floor. They built the mock-up and the two prototypes in this manner and were, after some time, able to get a production order from the RCAF for the CL-41A trainer, and somewhat later, from Malaysia, for the CL-41G counter-insurgency or ground-attack variant. Production of both versions did not pose any significant manufacturing problems for the company.

In 1962, with the CL-41 and the CL-44 in production, an entirely new program began;

license-manufacturing of the Lockheed F-104 fighter (Figs. 52, 53). This machine, with its Canadian-built version of the General Electric J-79 engines, was Canadair's first truly supersonic airplane. It was built at Canadair in quantity for the RCAF as well as for the U.S. Mutual Aid Program for NATO countries.

The fuselage was of surprisingly conventional construction, in aluminum and stainless steel, as was the empennage. One feature the F-104 inherited from the T-33 was the centre-fuselage being assembled from two halves, split on the centre line, which facilitated installation of wiring and equipment on the assembly line. The really curious feature, particularly for a supersonic fighter, was the razor-blade thin, unswept wings, each only 8 feet in span-wise length, for a total span of only 21 feet. These wings, however, required a good deal of careful machining, with both surfaces being tapered, and the multi-spar structure ending in five machined forgings that were the wing pick-up

points. Span-wise, there were only three ribs, and the leading edge of the wing could be 'drooped' by a hydraulic system, while the trailing edge featured ailerons, each moved by 10 actuators buried in the thickness of the slender wing. It had electrically-actuated inboard flaps. Because there was no volume for fuel in a wing with a 3.4 percent thickness-chord ratio, fuel lines ran out to the 200-gallon tanks at each wing tip. The flaps, by the way, incorporated a feature whereby compressor-bleed air was ejected through a series of slots on the upper surface of the flaps. Then as the flaps descended, a supersonic flow of air increased the effectiveness of the flaps and reduced the landing speed substantially. Some problems had to be overcome to make the slotted tubes, essential to this system.

Manufacture of the complex bifurcated inlet ducts, with shock-forming ramps and boundary-layer bleed, was much more complex than the simple inlet of the Sabre. A good deal of chemical milling of the duct skins was required and some very complex tooling.

Perhaps this is a good point to describe a few basic principles employed in the course of four of the next five Canadair programs. Much mention has been made of sheet-metal airplanes. The construction is based upon basic sheet metal, usually aluminum, but sometimes stainless steel or titanium. The metal was bent on a brake press, formed in a drop hammer or a hydro-forming press, or even stretched on a stretch press. It was then trimmed to shape, heat-treated and painted as a finished detail part ready to go into a sub-assembly. The essence of processing sheet-metal parts is that the parts are formed to shape without removal of metal from the surfaces except to trim to shape. This was the most common of all processes from the Northrop Delta to the North Star and the T-33, and the way the majority of the F-86 parts were made. In some cases, rather than starting with sheet metal, the parts started as extrusions, which could be bent, rolled, stretched, or otherwise formed, then trimmed ~ but again, without removing material except for trimming.

We now come to the second method, which is taking a billet, a bar, or a plate of metal, and machining away metal until the part achieves the right shape. This method is often referred to as "hogging-out". In some cases, up to 90% of the metal is removed. A noted sculptor of animal figures once said that he took a block of marble, then chiselled away everything that didn't look like a horse! Now, metal can be removed by a fixed tool, as a spoon would scrape butter from a block. This is exemplified by the lathe, the slotter, the broach, or the planer. The other method is to remove material with a rotating cutter, as with a saw, a drill, or a milling machine.

When metal is being removed from a heavy plate of metal, the piece is clamped to the table, and the table moves towards the cutting tool, removing a section of material along the length of the table. This is called the X axis. Successive cuts are made across the table, which is the Y axis. With the cut completed right across the plate, the cutting tool is lowered downwards for the second set of cuts, and this downwards move is called the Z axis. The Z axis is always the one passing through the axis of the cutter.

We can now change over to do the same operation on a milling machine with a rotating cutter, and do what is called 3-axis conventional machining. This is how the F-86 and F-104 wing skins were made. In practice, the method is a little more complex, as the cutters can move in two, or even three, axes simultaneously. For example, if the cutter moves along the X axis, and simultaneously moves downwards with the Z axis, the plate will be tapered, as is necessary for a wing skin. In some cases, the Z axis can be done in a series of steps to have the skin thicker where ribs are to be attached, and thinner elsewhere. The same 3-axis machining can also leave raised portions running span-wise as stiffeners, or integral stringers, which will save riveting stringers to the skin later, and simplifying sealing in a 'wet-wing'.

Up to this time, conventional 2-axis and 3-axis machining had been sufficient for Canadair's purposes, but the increasing need for parts that were 'machined-all-over' necessitated more advanced technology in machining, so that identical parts could be made in substantial quantity at lower costs.

One method was to go to three-spindle machines that made three identical parts, side by side, on the same machine, and with one operator. This could mean, of course, that all three parts were good, or that all three were unacceptable, so the solution was to make the milling of parts less susceptible to operator error. In 1963, therefore, Canadair began converting some conventional vertical milling machines to hydraulically operated 3-dimensional profilers, where a stylus followed the shape of an accurate model of the part, and a rotating cutter reproduced an identical part from a block of metal affixed to the bed of the machine. This was essentially similar in principle to the Keller machine that had been procured for the tool department in 1949, but the same principle was now to apply using such a machine for production of parts.

The next step was to convert three planer-type milling machines in the same manner, so that quite large skins could be machined, in quantity, to varying thickness and to the desired peripheral shape. At first, the plates were clamped to the bed of the machine, but, later on, a simple rubber 'O' ring around the periphery and a vacuum beneath the part, held it in place effectively without the risk of milling into the clamps, as happened on occasion. The machines had to have the appropriate speed range, of course, for speeds to cut aluminum are very much greater than those to cut steel.

To keep our chronological sequence, we will break away to consider another aircraft, which, apart from being only the second original Canadair design, was also a bold and original approach to combining the best features of the traditional fixed-wing aircraft with the characteristics of the helicopter.

This was the CL-84 vertical take-off and landing (VTOL) aircraft. The characteristics are described elsewhere, but, although the structure was generally conventional in order to keep cost down, there were some interesting manufacturing problems involved. The design included installation of ejection seats for the crew ~ fortunately, as it later turned out.

The manufacture and installation of the VTOL features of the CL-84 were all new to Canadair, of course. The engine was new, and the oil and fuel system had to work equally well when horizontal or vertical. A sturdy hinge was required so that the wing, together with the engines, could rise to the vertical while the fuselage stayed horizontal. Complex shafting had to link the two engines ~ in case one failed

while the machine was hovering, and also to transmit power to the tail rotor. There was also the hydraulic system to actuate the tilting of the wings, as well as the horizontal portion of the empennage.

Perhaps one of the most complex units to make was the 'mixing box' that received the output of the pilot's controls. This was necessary because, for instance, the aircraft would be banked by use of the ailerons while in normal horizontal flight, but by differential control of the pitch of the two propellers when in hover. Similarly, while turn was normally caused by rudder movement, in hover it was caused by the deflection of the ailerons, acted upon by the propeller slipstream. Finally, the climb and dive were caused by elevator deflection, but in hover they were caused by the increase or decrease of thrust of the tail rotor.

The most demanding of all was that, as control authority was transferred from one system to the other, it had to be done progressively and smoothly. In other words, if the pilot wanted to bank and turn, he would move the stick and rudder bars, and the mixing box would move the appropriate knobs, levers and control surfaces to meet the pilot's wishes. All this, and the other unusual requirements, had to be achieved with a very high degree of reliability. A total of four CL-84's were built at Canadair, but the fourth was never flown. Regrettably, the type never went into full production, even though it achieved all the goals set by the designers, and performed much better than several machines built later to the same general requirements by other manufacturers.

The next major program to come to Canadair was not an airplane, but several parts of an airplane. It was the F-111 fighter bomber (Fig. 54) designed by General Dynamics, the then parent company of Canadair. What made the program so important was that the design necessitated a great deal of new machinery, new processes and entry into a very different field for Canadair ~ the machining of complex parts in high-strength steel.

The F-111 featured a wing that pivoted so that the outer wings could be swept back for high speed flight, and swept forward for landing and takeoff. The pivot feature was based upon a large carry-through structure that was the centre section of the wing. This consisted of fully-machined upper and lower plates of high strength D6AC steel, which became the top and bottom of a box structure. This terminated either side in a large bearing, each of which was a pivot about which the outer wings could be moved by a system of hydraulic actuators. Canadair was also responsible for production of the pivot fittings that were built into the outer wing to mate with the bearings in the carry-through fitting. There were four of these pivot fittings ~ an upper and a lower part in the port wing, and a similar pair ~ but of the opposite hand ~ in the starboard wing. A good deal of tooling was therefore required, both milling fixtures and patterns to guide the stylus on the tracer-type machines that would be used. The D6AC steel, by the way, was rough cut up to 150,000 psi, and finishing operations were done in a hardness range up to 240,000 psi.

To make the carry-through fittings, a Cincinnati-Hypo and a Bertram 2-spindle machine were converted to hydraulic tracer-controlled 3-dimensional profilers. Similarly converted was a Giddings & Lewis open-side planer to 3-D profiling. This was also a two-spindle machine, so the carry-through fittings could be milled 'two-up'. These fittings, as well as being machined on all surfaces, had integral stringers milled in place, so that the finished part weighed only 675 pounds, while the original billet weighed 6,800 pounds. Some 90% of the material had been removed!

The outer wing pivot fittings, also in D6-AC steel, necessitated purchase of new machines of a type not on the market. Procurement was therefore initiated on what was to total 14 machines: two 4-spindle and twelve 6-spindle Wilsons. With these, up to six parts could be three-dimensionally profiled at the same time from a single pattern. The parts would then be flipped over and mounted in fixtures on the next machine to be machined on the other side.

On the same program, Canadair was also responsible for design, tooling and manufacturing of the fin and rudder. Both posed problems and need for new equipment, as the fin skins required tapering in several steps. This was accomplished at first by up to 14 stages of chemical milling, and also by a 'waffle-pattern' of stiffeners, where all the pockets had to be machined out of aluminum plate to close tolerances.

This was accomplished by an ingenious use of radial-arm routers that cut the pockets below while guided by a stylus in a pattern mounted immediately above the part. The skins, when assembled to the spars, had to be sealed carefully, as the fin was also a fuel tank. The rudder consisted of aluminum skins over an aluminum honeycomb core, so more tooling was required. The technology to stabilize and hold the core while machining it to shape was developed with the use of 'bacon-slicers' ~ toothless, mushroom-shaped high-speed cutters.

Finally, the core and skins were coated with the appropriate adhesives in the clean room, bagged, and then bonded into a single unit in one of the large autoclaves. Some hundreds of ship-sets of all the above F-111 parts were shipped to Fort Worth, Texas, and subsequently, a later and much modified vertical stabilizer was supplied for the EF-111 at Grumman.

As can be seen, while this was a sub-contract job for aircraft parts, the program had a profound effect on Canadair's level of technology and range of capability.

With the conversion from conventional type to tracer-type machining in hand for the F-111 program, Canadair had to start planning for an even greater move forward as numerical control machines came on the scene. The first step was procurement, in 1963, of three Pratt & Whitney Tape-o-Matic drilling machines, then two N/C Warner & Swasey turret lathes, followed by two Kearney & Trecker 3-axis machining centres with a 'ready-use' capacity of 15 tools, then two Cincinnati CIM-X machining centres in 1967. New additions were three K&T Model 814's ~ 3-spindle, 3-axis machines; the first of the 5-axis machines; and a group of three single-spindle K&T Model III machines that included such refinements as a 'ready-use' capacity for 15 tools, circular inter-polation and cutter compensation.

Before going further, we can look back to the earlier conventional and tracer-type controls, where the machines could make cuts in three axes, X, Y, and Z. Now we are talking of 5-axis machining. The fourth axis is accomplished by rocking the entire cutting head, or heads, progressively as the cutters move along the bed of the machine, the X-axis, gradually tilting more and more as the cutters move forward, so that the vertical cut moves from the vertical to give a bevelling cut, known as a 'swarfing cut'. This movement is in the A axis. At the end of the cut, it may be necessary to take a bevel cut across the width of the table, along the Y-axis. For this, the cutter heads must tilt for the cross-cut ~ this is the B axis. As the cut moves from travelling along the bed, feeding in X and A axes simultaneously, the cutters must then start moving around the corner and, for a period, they will also be moving in the Y and B axes as well as the X and A.

These complex cuts, of course, could only be accomplished under tape control. But by such a method, the most complex parts can be cut once the tape is proven, reliably and economically, particularly if three cutting heads are making three identical parts simultaneously.

Capability such as this requires, of course, backup of a lot of equipment and training of people. Canadair had purchased a Gerber N/C drafting machine to supplement the old lofting method, and had hired and trained personnel to make the mylar tapes that control movement of the machines in 2-axis, 3-axis or up to 5-axis operations. There were also expenditures for pre-set tools and adapters, development of the computers and training of operators.

With all this planning well in hand, Canadair started bidding on a number of very large subcontract packages for parts of the Lockheed C-5A transport aircraft (Fig. 55). With the winning of some of the contracts, it was necessary to expand the company's clean-room facilities, procure larger autoclaves (12-foot and 15-foot diameter and 40-feet in length) and a large new stretch press. There was also the need to train personnel to handle the very large honeycomb-bonded structures of the C-5A main landing gear fairings and doors, and the aft cargo doors. Another contract for the wing leading-edge and slats and the ailerons, necessitated greater 5-axis machining capabil-

ity, so six very large Cincinnati three-spindle, 5-axis machines were procured and installed in two groups of three machines, end-to-end. This meant that, with three of the 3-spindle gantries mounted above a 140-foot long bed, setup could be proceeding at one end, while two or even three gantries were cutting parts 'three-up' further along the bed.

The C-5A program, therefore, was of great importance to Canadair, running over several years, and in spite of the huge change traffic, as Lockheed tried to build the airplanes at the same time as design was proceeding, it was ultimately profitable, and brought the factory capability up to a very high level. In fact, several future programs such as the F-15 subcontract and the complex Challenger program relied very much on the equipment and skills developed for the C-5A subcontract.

One of the packages Canadair won was the C-5A wing tips, but there were even greater problems than with the other packages, and many changes. Few who were involved will forget the attempts to manufacture the 'little canoe' and in the end, Lockheed took the package back and found they had to redesign before the parts could be manufactured.

Another noteworthy item was depleted uranium for aileron balance weights, although these were not to be machined, simply bolted into the assembly. It was necessary to purchase an electron-beam welding unit, which welded the C-5A slat tracks in a vacuum chamber. There was also the requirement, new to Canadair, to use very expensive titanium fasteners that necessitated a considerable amount of training of personnel.

Then there were problems with the paper-thin (.012") outer skins on the landing gear fairings. It transpired that stones flung up from the 28 wheels punctured these thin skins, so heavier material had to be used.

For all the problems, the C-5A kept the Canadair tooling and manufacturing shops busy for some time, and resulted in much new technology and new equipment that was to be used on later programs.

With the CL-41 in production, and with the F-111 and C-5A subcontract programs moving ahead, Canadair was awarded a contract for the license production of the Northrop F-5 fighter – for Canada as the CF-5, and for the Netherlands as the NF-5. What looked like a simple, lightweight fighter, proved to be much more than that, as the F-5 was quite a complex machine to build. The fuselage, while of relatively conventional construction, was 'area-ruled' so there were many complex curved surfaces to form, as well as the supporting structure and the bifurcated inlet ducts that led to twin-engines. The wing skins were tapered and machined all over with electrically actuated leading and trailing edge devices. There were 'hard points' for a wide range of stores, and provision for in-flight refuelling. The aft-fuselage and 'boat-tail' featured a very high parts-count, with fully formed, light-gauge titanium parts that necessitated purchase of a hot-forming and sizing press, a first application for Canadair. At this time, 1968, a new 41,000-ton Verson direct-acting hydraulic press was purchased for this and other programs. One unusual feature was the construction of the horizontal tail surfaces, which pivoted on a machined forging, 'the shotgun-fitting'. The structure consisted of a pair of skins supported by full-depth aluminum honeycomb, with only a small leading and trailing edge member and a root rib, all autoclave bonded.

Another Canadair project that was also in production at the same time as the CL-41 and CF-5 and the other subcontracts, was the inimitable CL-215 (Fig. 56), the Water Bomber. Canadair, having inherited a tradition of building flying boats, actually began their design studies for a fire-fighting aircraft with a twin-boom float plane, the CL-204, but as studies continued, the design crystallized into a conventional flying boat that would have looked good on the line at Canadian Vickers. Because the company never expected to get any substantial production rate for what was, literally, a flying fire engine, the manufacturing was done on what is known as 'soft-tooling' to keep costs down.

This was a good decision at the time, but one that was to cause many problems further along the line. The CL-215 entered production in 1967, and was still being produced, albeit much modified, almost 30 years later. As to the need for capital equipment, because Canadair had designed the machine as a low-cost project, it was to be made with existing facilities and minimum tooling. But the large wing, of 93-foot span, justified a large Drivematic unit for handling and riveting automatically. The design included a good deal of fibreglass and honeycomb structure for wing tips, flaps, water tanks, and various doors, all of which could be produced with existing equipment. The problems of manufacturing the two water-drop doors, which were hogged-out of aluminum plate, were overcome by making a pattern, and then tracer-milling them on the Wilson profilers. Otherwise, the very conventional structure of the CL-215 presented few problems.

The next job, however, did pose many problems and little return on company investment. This was the subcontract manufacture of wing panels, vertical stabilizers, engine pylons, slat tracks, and detail points for the Dassault 'Mercure', as well as some wing panels for the Falcon 10 business jet. The program necessitated installation of a vapour-blast system, which was used to blast the surface of the machined parts with glass beads to introduce compression into the surfaces to resist fatigue cracking. This was to replace the normal Canadair Pangborn system that used air and cast steel shot, and seemed to offer no apparent advantages. There was also a requirement for broaching and burnishing of holes that meant more equipment

and training that didn't pay off ~ not more than 10 Mercures were ever built. One novel feature was the forming of the aerofoil in the heavy skins by 'bump forming', using a big, recently acquired, Pacific brake press.

One more successful subcontract, begun in 1975, was manufacture of a number of bulkheads for the MacDonnell F-15 aircraft (Fig. 57). From modest beginnings, the program grew to include a number of very complex 5-axis aluminum and titanium bulkheads, which fitted well, two-up and three-up, on our Cincinnati profilers, keeping the machines working over a fairly slack period.

In 1976, a large subcontract came into Canadair involving manufacture of parts for the Lockheed P-3C as Canadian Content for the Canadian version, the Aurora, as well as for the U.S. version, the Orion. The P-3C had been developed from the Lockheed L-188 Electra, once a competitor of the CL-44, so it represented construction of the late 1950s. It required little new except a fairly sophisticated tooling setup with Drivematic riveting for the wing panels and a lot of work for the plastic shop with the radomes and MAD booms. There were also some conventional fuselage sections, as well as the electrical load centres, to provide work for those shops until the next big Canadair program got under way.

On 29 October 1976, came the decision to commence tooling, planning, procurement, and construction of what was to become the CL-600 Challenger aircraft (Fig. 58) and its derivatives. Because of the new equipment purchased, and the technologies developed on the F-111 and the C-5A contracts, together with the solid production background described briefly above, Canadair had all that was necessary to design and produce the Challenger. The design included fully machined skins, spars and ribs, a conventional fuselage structure that incorporated many machined fittings, a good deal of metal-to-metal and honeycomb bonding, full

pressurization, and integral tanks. There was also, as always, something new. In the case of the Challenger, composite materials, particularly the graphite-epoxy type, demanded attention, as did the instrumentation of the cockpit that was being upgraded to newer concepts. All this, the old and the new, was supported by highly developed tooling and planning, estimating and scheduling capability, in addition to the engineering and experimental testing skills that would be proven as the Challenger went through the next very difficult years. Even a minimum description of the production process to produce a Challenger would merit a volume to itself. Perhaps, in time, it will be written.

Missing from this account is the part played by many departments that are seldom in the limelight: accounting, contracts, data processing, expediting, liaison, material control, material and processes, N/C programming, outside production, preliminary design, plant engineering, procurement, product support, production control, personnel, maintenance, quality control, stores, and shipping and receiving. These, and others, were essential services without which production shops could not function. At Canadair, there was a direct line that ran from the young graduate with a digital-readout pyrometer calibrated to national standards, to Ed Forrest with his blowtorch, heating the material until the spots of oil turned brown, or equally from the N/C programmer to the shipyard worker laying out lines on the lofting floor.

It's over a hundred years since the Wright brothers, but there is still a requirement for the best of people in order to produce the most competitive of products.

1. Canadian Vickers Shipyard with three Vedettes in the 'air harbour', about 1928. At the lower right is the floating drydock, 'Duke of Connaught,' and an FC-2 on the St. Lawrence River.

2. Launching of first Viking IV built at Canadian Vickers. G-CYEU. 25 July 1923

J. HAYWARD MONTREAL

EU. CVI. #1047 July 25 1923

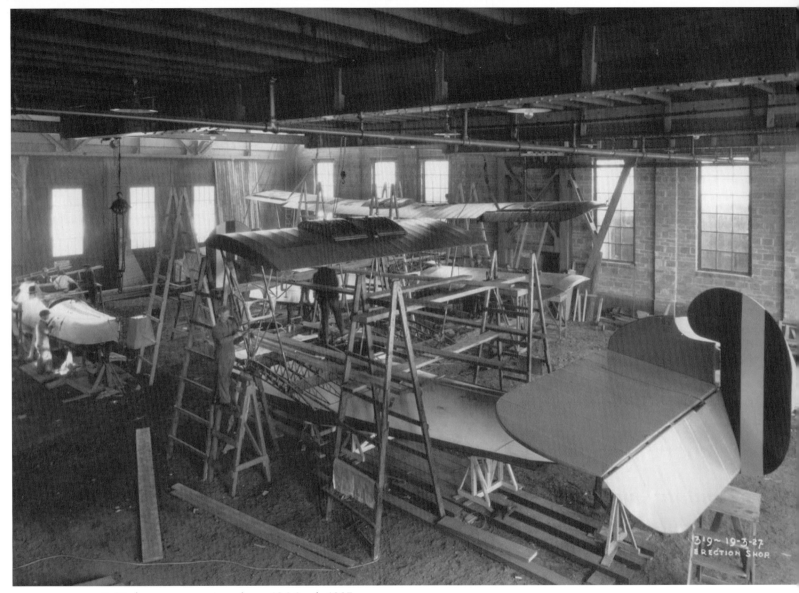

3. Vedette construction shop. 19 March 1927

4. Vedette I prototype converted to Wright J-4
power. In background, a Viking IV. 22 May 1925

5. Vedette hull under construction, keel down.
19 September 1924

6. Vedette wings under construction

7. Vedette VA: Installation of Lynx engine on
final line. 1930

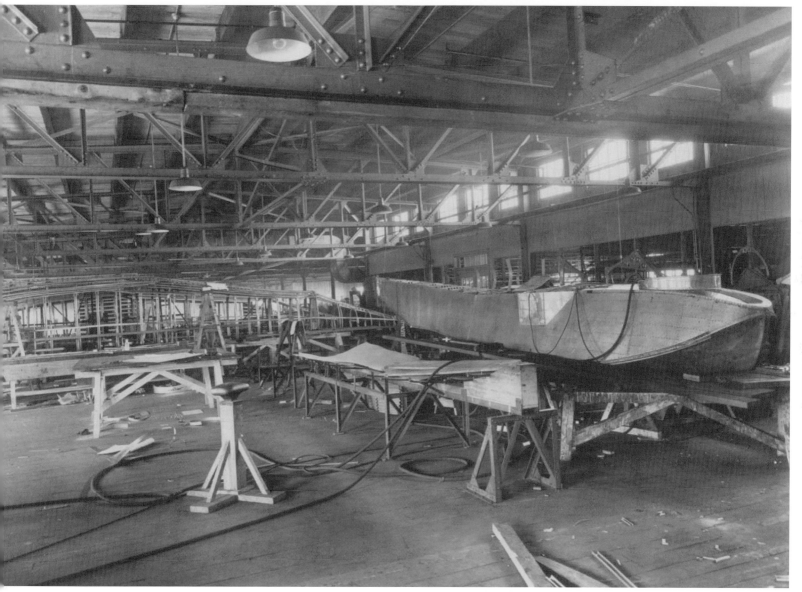

8. First metal Vedette hull.
At left, Vancouver hull, built keel up. 1930

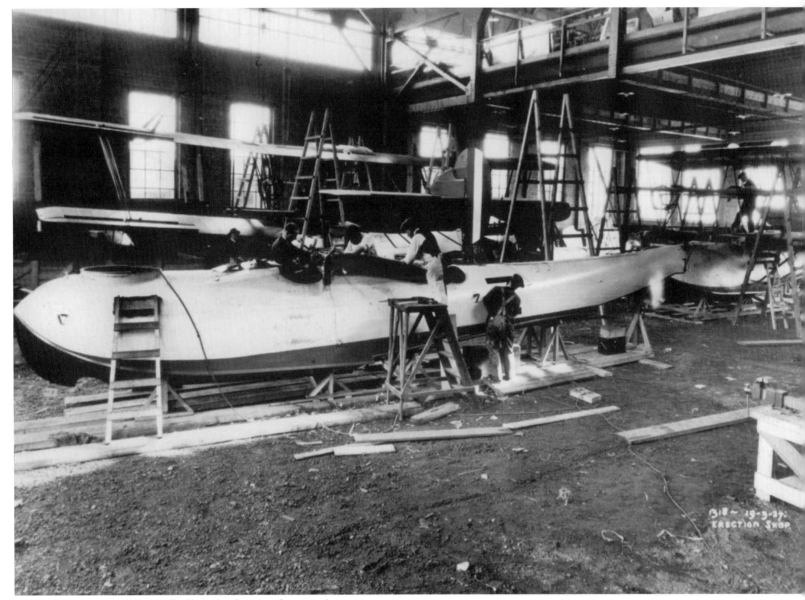

9. Varuna hull. In background, two other
Varunas being assembled. 19 March 1927

10. Vista prototype, with Genet engine and cradle. Note external stiffening beads along hull. Right, American-built Fokker Universal G-CASF brought in for overhaul

VISTA 13009,
28ᵗʰ NOV. 1927.

11. Vista in the 'Air Harbour' near floating
drydock. 28 November 1927

12. Velos prototype, P&W Wasp Engines

13. Avro 504N float plane G-CYGK, modified
with Wright J-4 engine. 1925

14. Three Avro 504N land planes and the Vigil prototype under construction. 1 February 1928

15. Avro 552 prototype, Wolseley Viper engine, with early land plane undercarriage with central skid. Second fuselage and centre section in foreground. 19 November 1924

16. Canadian Vickers Air Harbour, 17 August 1928, with FC-2 'Razorback' G-CYXU, the Velos prototype amd two American-built Fokker aircraft ~ the Super Universal G-CASK of Punch Dickens and the Standard Universal G-CASF.

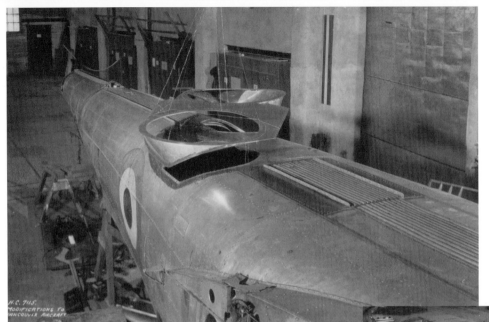

17. Vancouver IIS. Hull modifications for gun-ring mounts and added walkway for mooring

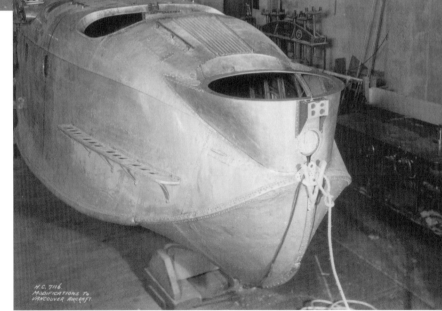

18. Second Fokker Super Universal, CF-AFM
built by Canadian Vickers. Edo floats.

19. Northrop Delta I prototype on floats and
beaching gear. Wright Cyclone engine.

20. Northrop Delta MK-I prototype

21. Northrop Delta MK–II, CV684 (RCAF 01)
with wheeled undercarriage

22. The twelfth Stranraer CF-BYA, partially masked for painting.

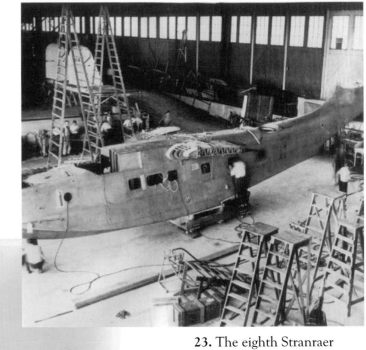

23. The eighth Stranraer
CF-GYH (later NR 45389
and later still VP-JAJ).

23. Canadian Vickers Supermarine
Stranraer, fabric covering removed

24. Canadian Vickers Supermarine Stranraer prototype, CV-184 (RCAF 907) CF-BY1

25. Canadian Vickers-built Consolidated OA-10A
    for the U.S. Navy

26. Canso A/OV-10A fuselage assembly line,
1943. Note that first positions are inverted.

27A. Canadair, 12 August 1949, 1800 Laurentian Blvd, St. Laurent, next to runway 24 of Cartierville Airport.. The streetcar tracks are to the right and parallel to the boulevard. Wartime housing, fondly known as "Dogpatch," top right. CN tracks beyond Bois Franc, top of photo. Curtiss-Reid aviation and the Flying Club, upper left. Restaurant (greasy spoon) in centre. North Star pushed from runway up to Bldg 106.

27B Canadair, late 1950s. Runway 24 still there before being grassed over. Curtiss-Reid and Laurentide Aviation at right. Plants 2 and 4 across the field. Addition of run-up installations at end of runway 28, material warehouses, flight hangar, and other buildings. Note full parking lots.

27c. Canadair DC-4M1 North Star: installation
of Rolls-Royce Merlin 620 power plants. 1946

28. Canadair Argonaut built for BOAC

29. Laying out CL-28 lines on the lofting floor.

30. Plaster masters. The outer surfaces represent the skin inside mouldline. Drop-hammer, press and stretch-form tools can be made directly or indirectly from the plaster masters.

31. Keller 3-D
tracer mill
making
T-33 nose
door tool

32. Canadair Sabre 3, the only one built.
Orenda 3 engine.

33. Sabre 5 production line in Building 202,
Canadair, Plant 2

34. Canadair Sabre 6 (Orenda 14) and
the little cabin we built for use during testing

35. Basic Sabre sub-assembly,
inlet duct with cockpit above.

Workers boarding the streetcar

36. Workers leaving Plant 1.
   Note the little restaurant to the right.

37. Their Royal Highnesses sign the Canadair
guest book in Plant 1, 30 October 1951.

38. The Canadair T-33 ANX prototype with
Rolls-Royce Nene 10 engine (RCAF 21001)

39. T-33AN Repair & Overhaul line in Plant 4.
Note fin of aircraft 21006, the sixth Canadian T-33.

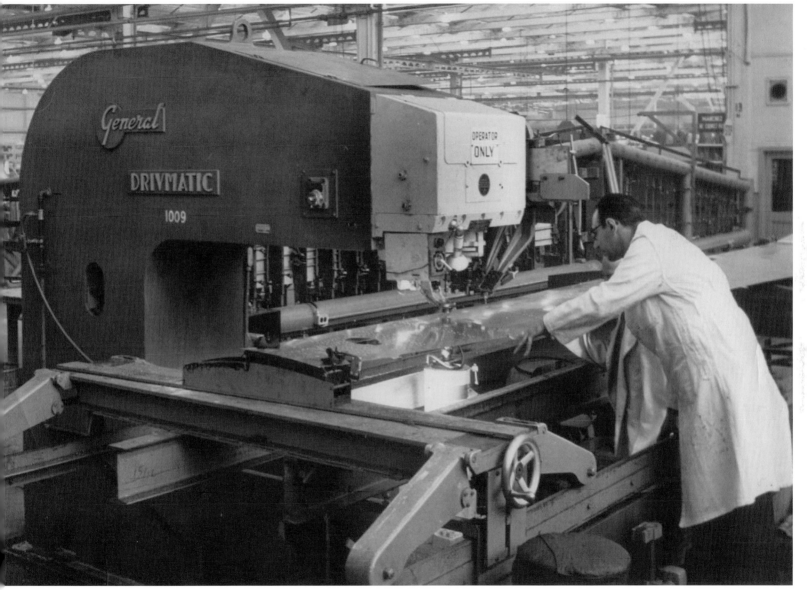

40. Drivematic automatic riveting machine with T-33 skin panel.

41. Boeing B-47 (N° 51-2051) arrives at
Cartierville. 16 February 1956

42. The Boeing B-47 modified and
instrumented to test the Avro Iroquois engine

43. Canadair CL-28-1 Argus

44. Canadair Ltd. in its heyday, circa 1955, with Plant 1 in foreground, Plant 2 across the field and Plant 4 top right. Main runway extended.

45. CL-28 wing outer panel assembly fixture.
Note optical tool alignment equipment.

46. Canadair CL-44-6 (Yukon) fuselage
assembly fixtures.

47. Canadair CL-44-D4 swing-tail for
Slick Airways

48. CL-44 D4 final assembly (centre); two CL-44-6 noses, and one CL-44 D4 (left); a CL-44-6 and a CL-66 (background) in Building 117.

49. Mock-up of the Canadair CL-41 trainer aircraft

50. C1-41 rear fuselage sub-assembly line.

51. Fred Phillips, designer of the CL-41, and
test pilot Ian MacTavish prepare for a flight.

52. Canadair CF-104 (Orenda-built GE-J79
engine) for the RCAF

53. CF-104 centre fuselage, split on centre line at this stage.

54. F-111 subcontract.
Wing carry-through fitting (above)
Pivot fitting (above right)
and fin skin (right).

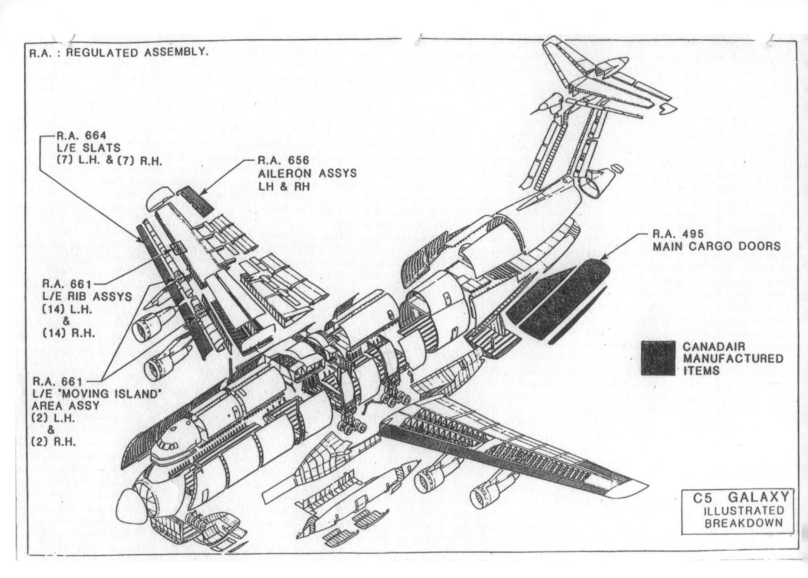

R.A. : REGULATED ASSEMBLY.

R.A. 664
L/E SLATS
(7) L.H. & (7) R.H.

R.A. 656
AILERON ASSYS
LH & RH

R.A. 495
MAIN CARGO DOORS

R.A. 661
L/E RIB ASSYS
(14) L.H.
&
(14) R.H.

CANADAIR
MANUFACTURED
ITEMS

R.A. 661
L/E 'MOVING ISLAND'
AREA ASSY
(2) L.H.
&
(2) R.H.

C 5 GALAXY
ILLUSTRATED
BREAKDOWN

55. C-5A Galaxy - Illustrated breakdown

56. CL-215 final line. Wing mating to fuselage and final fuselage assembly.

57. F-15 Sub
contract: 5-
axis machined
wing carry-
through fitting.

58. Canadair CL-600 Challenger: prototype and
follow-on production on assembly line. 1978

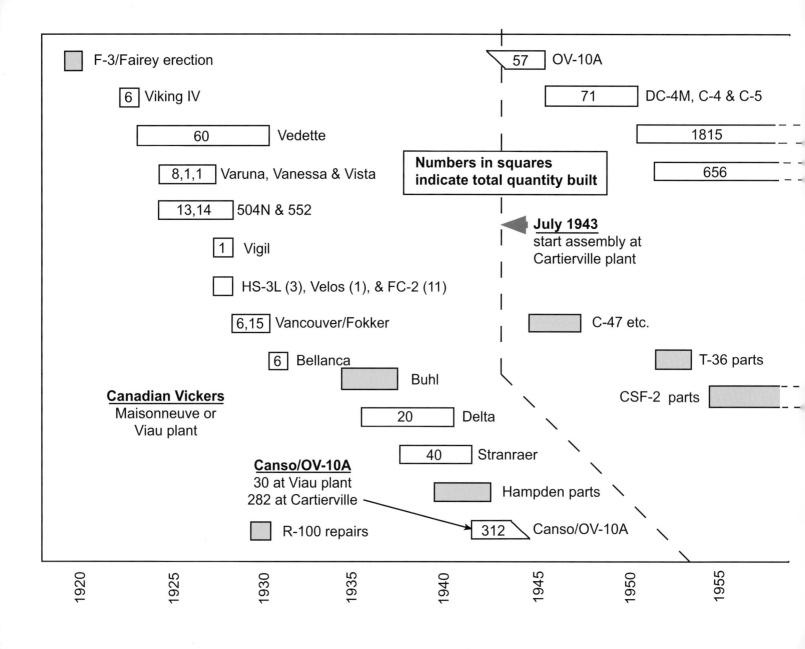

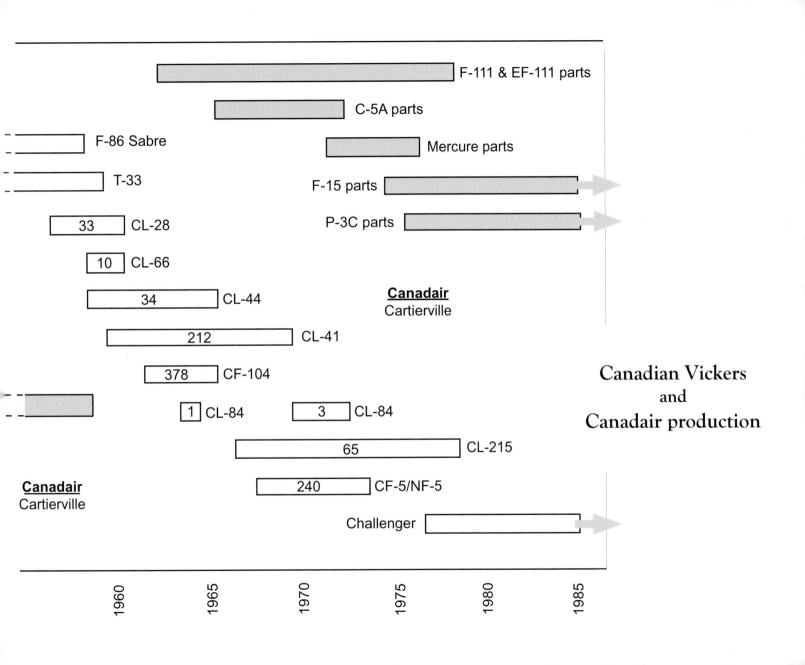

F-111 & EF-111 parts

C-5A parts

F-86 Sabre

Mercure parts

T-33

F-15 parts

33 CL-28

P-3C parts

10 CL-66

34 CL-44

212 CL-41

Canadair
Cartierville

378 CF-104

Canadian Vickers
and
Canadair production

1 CL-84   3 CL-84

65 CL-215

Canadair
Cartierville

240 CF-5/NF-5

Challenger

1960   1965   1970   1975   1980   1985

GLOSSARY

Americanizing. Revision of European design utilizing North American materials and fasteners to achieve an equivalent part or assembly.

Annealing. Process by which metals are heat-treated to make them soft and ductile prior to the forming process.

Anodizing. Chemical conversion treatment that protects metal from corrosion.

Autoclave. Large vessel in which aircraft parts are loaded and assembled with appropriate adhesives in place, so that a combination of heat and pressure can be applied until the adhesives are cured and the parts removed. Heating can be by steam, natural gas or electrical power.

Bostick. Proprietary sealant used to make a hull water-tight or to seal potential air leaks in a pressurized fuselage.

Bucker. Second member of a team of riveters. The first places a rivet in a hole and holds the riveting gun against the head of the rivet while the *bucker* holds a steel *buck* against the far side of the rivet, acting as an anvil and forming the other end of the rivet to shape.

Cantilever. Wing or structure that has no external bracing; all forces are carried within the structure.

Carriage builders. The highly skilled builders of strong, yet light, carriages that can readily be pulled by horses, or technicians skilled in the use of wood, metal, leather, and fabric; also called coach builders.

Chemical milling. The process of lowering aircraft parts into tanks of liquid. Certain portions of the parts are bare metal and are attacked by the liquid, which removes the metal at a known rate. Other areas of the parts are masked off by a rubber-like coating, and they are not affected. In this way, the weight of parts can be reduced by removing material that is unnecessary, and leaving material that is required to give the part structural strength, or where the material needs a certain thickness for fasteners to be installed.

Compass swing. An aircraft is placed on a flat surface, then rotated to all the cardinal points of the compass. A chart is then prepared for the pilot's reference showing how much variation there is between the actual readings and the true readings.

Complex machining. Further refining of four-axis machining can include:

<u>circular interpolation.</u> The cutter programmed to cut around a circular path with no pivot at the centre.

<u>cutter compensation.</u> The progressive wear of the cutter is established and the cutter moves forward accordingly.

<u>multi-spindle machining.</u> Machine with a broader bed so that two or even three parts can be loaded and machined simultaneously by two or three or even more cutters controlled by a central computer.

Dirigible. A word from the French meaning *controllable.* A balloon simply drifts downwind. Dirigible airships have a source of power on board, so can be directed or steered in any desired direction.

Dope. Form of cellulose acetate liquid, usually coloured, applied to fabric for strength and durability, and stretching the fabric taut after being stitched in place. Dope was also applied to wood structures.

Duralumin. Alloy of aluminium that contains copper, commonly used in aircraft construction

Empennage. From the French meaning the tail portion of an aircraft, usually consisting of the fin, rudder, horizontal stabilizer, elevators, and, in some cases, the extreme end of the fuselage.

Fairings. Generally non-structural portions of the external surfaces of an aircraft added to streamline the airflow and reduce drag.

Family of tools. Set of tools designed and built to accomplish a series of operations, such as a set of tools to trim a piece of flat sheet metal to a required shape, then to form the metal to desired contour, then to drill holes in the required places so that parts can be assembled to adjacent parts.

Fatigue. Failure of a metal part due to the continuous application of a force, below the limit to cause failure in a short time but sufficient to cause failure over a very long period of time.

Fitters and riggers. Fitters are what today would be called mechanics. Riggers would be the workers employed to install and set up the standing and running rigging of a sailing ship. For aircraft, the riggers are skilled technicians who aligned the bracing of the aircraft's various parts so that the assembled aircraft would be stable in flight, and responsive to the movement of the control surfaces.

Fuselage. Body of an aircraft.

Heat treatment. Process to temper or harden material after it has been formed to shape.

Hogging-out. Machining away metal from a solid block until the desired shape is achieved.

Hydro-forming. Forming parts in metal on a hydraulic press.

Intercostals. Members running between one structural member and another.

Joiner. Skilled woodworker.

Keel. Strong structural member running fore and aft.

Keelson. Subsidiary keel member.

Keller. Machine capable of machining three-dimensional copies in metal of a three-dimensional model made of plaster or other material. Named after Helen Keller, who was both blind and deaf.

Kirksite. Alloy of tin and lead used to make drop-hammer dies or other tools used in forming metals.

Lathe. Machine tool that could be used to rotate pieces of wood or metal against a stationary cutter to make parts.

Lofting. Drawing of the full-scale layout of the outline and various cross-sections of a ship or an aircraft, traditionally on a wooden floor, so that parts can be cut or formed to the lines established. Also tooling, which can be made to conform to the lines. Originally, large pieces of wood were cut with an adz to conform to the loft-lines. Later, metal was formed on a tool made to such lines.

Longerons. Fore and aft structural members in a fuselage that carry the main structural loads. A form of multiple keels, usually together with lighter fore and aft stringers.

Machining. Process of removing metal from a block of material until the remaining material is of the desired shape and size. There are generally three methods of machining:

three-axis. Involves cutting in three planes: across the part, up and down the part, and in and out of the part. These are generally called the x, y and z axes with the z-axis always being the axis where the cutter moves further into the part, or withdraws from the part.

four-axis. Same as three-axis machining, but the cutter is able to swing as it cuts, and by progressively swinging as it cuts along a part, it achieves a *swarfing* cut, as along the length of a spar. This is generally known as the a-axis.

five-axis. Same as three-axis, but the cutter can swing or rock in two directions, and can be programmed to move in the three-axes noted above, while rocking the a-axis and simultaneously rocking the cutter in the b-axis, cutting continuously all the while. This means that virtually any three-dimensional shape can be machined out of a block of metal.

Master tool. Tool used to make other tools, particularly where the parts to be made must be interchangeable or replaceable.

Monocoque. From the French. A structure in which a large portion of the loads are carried by the external skin of metal, plywood or composite material, instead of the old fabric-covered structures where all loads were carried by the internal structure.

Nacelle. Separate body, usually containing the engines,

but a term once used for a body containing the pilot.

Nautical nomenclature.

bulkheads. Give shape, but pass right across the ship or aircraft, separating the various holds or cabins, with appropriate doors or openings.

keel. Strong and to which all other structure is attached.

ribs. Curved members giving transverse shape to a hull.

stringers. Light structural members that run from bow to stern, more or less parallel to the keel.

aft. Toward the stern.

athwartships. Across the width of a vessel.

forward. Towards the bow.

port. Left-hand side of a ship or aircraft, when one faces forward, toward the bow.

starboard. Originally *steer* board, the right-hand side when facing forward. Before the invention of the rudder, the steering oar was slung out-board on the right-hand side of the ship, hence *steer board.*

Offsets, waterlines, buttock lines. Old shipbuilding terms, still used for aircraft, to define, respectively, the distance that particular points were offset from the centreline of the ship. Water lines, even on aircraft, are a series of horizontal planes that, theoretically, pass through the hull. The third term, buttock lines, denotes the curved longitudinal sections of a hull that run parallel to the keel.

Planer. Machine with a moving table on which metal plate or parts are loaded. As the material moves back and forth, it passes under a fixed or rotating cutter, and successive passes leave a virtually flat surface on the material.

Plaster master. Basic tool made of a series of metal sheets cut to represent cross-sections of an aircraft, held apart by threaded rods then wrapped in wire mesh. Plaster is laid smoothly on this base until the external surface of the aircraft is produced.

Pressurization. System of pumping air under pressure into the fuselage so that the crew and the passengers can breathe normally when the aircraft is flying at great heights.

Profiler. Machine that cuts metal to a desired profile.

Quenching. Consists of dropping a heated metal part into cold water or oil to reduce its temperature abruptly. This treatment affects the microstructure of the material in such a way as to harden, soften or temper the part, depending on the type of metal being processed.

Ratetooling. Also known as duplicate tooling, these are additional tools used to increase the number of aircraft produced per week or per month.

Rigging boards. Wooden boards that could be attached to the wing of an aircraft, appropriately marked so that correct movement of the ailerons or flaps can be established and adjusted. Also, simliar boards used for rudders and elevators.

Salt bath. In order to heat metal to a relatively high temperature (400F to 1000F) for various uses, the pieces are dropped into a bath filled with salt in a liquid state, which achieves a far higher temperature than, for example, water, that boils at 100C (212F).

Splash. Plaster cast taken off a plaster master to achieve a 'female' mould as part of the tool-making process.

Spars. Major structural members in the wing of an aircraft, generally running from the fuselage out to the wing tip.

Splicing. Technique used to intertwine the separate strands of a rope or a wire cable to join cables or to form a bight or loop at the end of a cable.

Springback. Tendency of a material to move back toward its original shape after being bent or formed. It is therefore necessary to bend some materials a little beyond the desired angle so that they spring back to the desired angle.

Strain gauges. Very small pattern of small wires placed on a metal part to measure the strain (extension or compression of the part) when a load is applied. From the known strain or deformation, the stress in the part can be calculated.

Stretch-forming. Process whereby a machine stretches sheet metal or extrusions to a point beyond the limit of proportionality, but less than the breaking point. When the loads are removed, the part maintains the curvature or form of the tool on which it has been formed.

Stress-relieving. Heat treatment process used to relieve the stresses in a metal part. These stresses are caused during the forming of the parts.

Stringers. Lesser fore-and-aft or spanwise members that supplement the longerons or spars and give the external shape of the fuselage or wing.

Tooling terms.

fixture. Tool that holds a part during some manufacturing process but does not guide the cutter.

jig. Tool that has two distinct functions: one holds an aircraft part firmly and the other guides the cutter while that part is machined, drilled, milled, or assembled (see fixture).

Wet-wing. Wing made entirely of metal but sealed at all the joints so that the wing, or major parts of the wing, can be filled with fuel, rather than installing separate fuel tanks in the wing. The wet-wing saves weight and increases available volume for fuel.

INDEX

ABOUT THE AUTHOR

Patrick Campbell (P. Eng. Retd.) was born in Selkirk, Manitoba, in 1923 and was educated in Canada and in England. He was apprenticed to D. Napier & Son from 1940 to 1944 and was employed by the Royal Aircraft Establishment, Farnborough. He was next a disarmament officer with the Control Commission for Germany. This was followed by a year at the College of Aeronautics, Cranfield, and some time with the Bristol Aeroplane Co. (Engines Div.). He returned to Canada in 1952 and was employed by Canadair until 1984, then spent a further period, to 1997, on the Canadian Patrol Frigate program. Since 1999, Patrick has been involved in volunteer work with the Canadian Aviation Heritage Centre as Director of Manufacturing.

Other books by Patrick Campbell:
Shades of Sherlock (1999)
Tides of the Wight (1999)
Holmes in the West Country (2000)